ISBN 978-1-333-94558-9
PIBN 10687644

1 MONTH OF
FREE
READING

at
www.ForgottenBooks.com

By purchasing this book you are eligible for one month membership to ForgottenBooks.com, giving you unlimited access to our entire collection of over 700,000 titles via our web site and mobile apps.

To claim your free month visit:

www.forgottenbooks.com/free687644

English
Français
Deutsche
Italiano
Español
Português

www.forgottenbooks.com

Mythology Photography **Fiction**
Fishing Christianity **Art** Cooking
Essays Buddhism Freemasonry
Medicine **Biology** Music **Ancient**
Egypt Evolution Carpentry Physics
Dance Geology **Mathematics** Fitness
Shakespeare **Folklore** Yoga Marketing
Confidence Immortality Biographies
Poetry **Psychology** Witchcraft
Electronics Chemistry History **Law**
Accounting **Philosophy** Anthropology
Alchemy Drama Quantum Mechanics
Atheism Sexual Health **Ancient History**
Entrepreneurship Languages Sport
Paleontology Needlework Islam
Metaphysics Investment Archaeology
Parenting Statistics Criminology
Motivational

PHOTO. BY LEMMON.

Yours Truly

John C. McEldowney Jr.

....HISTORY....

—OF—

WETZEL COUNTY,

WEST VIRGINIA.

ɤ30

—BY—

JOHN C. McELDOWNEY, JR.

1901.

17737

PREFACE.

The History of Wetzel County runs from the year of 1772 to the present time. The author has used great pains in securing the most important events during that time, and has succeeded as far as the interesting matter is concerned, though there may be a few incidents left out for the want of data. The most important ones have been secured. There may be incidents in the history of the county that would not only speak bad of the morality of the county, but would bring back remembrances of unhappy days, and things that would sadden the pages of Wetzel's History. Wetzel county for years has been suffering with a name that she does not deserve, and she is gradually blotting it out. In the history of the county there are a great many men whose lives should have been mentioned in the book but were not, from the fact that the author could not secure anything concerning them. The author has put in four months in securing information and in writing this history. It does not require very much of an education to write a book of this kind. You can see that when glancing over the pages.

THE AUTHOR.

CONTENTS.

PREHISTORIC RACES OF WETZEL COUNTY.

The known history of this valley covers but a short period of time, probably 125 years, since the advent of the present race. The Indian at that time was its only inhabitant. He was not at all an industrious being, but a free man, whose home was wherever he chanced to place his wigwam. It is plain to be seen that a race more civilized and industrious inhabited this valley and the whole United States. Whether they were of the same race as the Indian, will never be known, but we do know that they were more thriving and industrious. The earth works that are found, in so many parts of this valley, are, no doubt, the works of a previous race. The stone implements, that are found in so many parts of this valley, are constructed out of a material that man at this genius world, deem not pliable. There was a mound, at one time, situated on the shore of the Ohio river, on the farm now owned by John C. McEldowney, a mound which was possessed of a rare antiquity. The following is a sketch taken from the January 19, 1901, edition of the Wheeling Register:

"The river bank below the fair grounds, opposite the amphitheatre, was possessed at one time of a mound, that was very antique. The mound, which is now part of the Ohio river, was at that time as high as the bank is to-day, it being very much isolated from the shore. It was often used as a place of resort, to boys from the years of 1840 to 1850. Samuel McEldowney at that time lived near the spot, where the mound was situated. Many stone hatchets, tomahawks, spears, necklaces, earrings, arrow heads and many other curiosities were

taken from the mound.   But one of the things that was of so
vast importance, and no doubt was greatly admired in prehisto-
ric times, was a golden image of an unknown god, moulded out
of pure gold, without a mixture of any other metalic elements.
It was about ten inches high, having a base, as though it were
an ornament, and moulded on it was a statue of an unknown
god.   If the image could have talked it could tell a history of
itself, that no doubt would unravel the mystery of the pre-his-
toric races.   It was found by the late Capt. Robert McEldowney.   Willis De Haas, an antiquarian and agent for the Smithsonian institute, was then writing a history of the border wars
of Western Virginia, and borrowed the curiosity.   Comments
of all kinds were passed on it by all of the leading newspapers
of that day.   The president of the Smithsonian institute au-
thorized De Haas to purchase the image at any price, if possible, but the prices offered were refused.   The image was
then borrowed by one Phenton McCabe, who disappeared from
this place as soon as he had the image in his possession.   A
half moon moulded of copper was found near the same mound
and about the same time by Mrs. Geo. Martin.   Copper wrist-
bands were found in a rock mound situated near the water
tanks at New Martinsville.   Are these the works of the Indian?   If it be answered by ones who have lived with the Indians all their life, they would say no, for they have never
seen them constructing such articles as we have just mentioned.

THE INDIANS.

The Indian race is the most peculiar of the living races; their origin is not known, and ideas of all kinds have been expressed on their origin by noted historians. We can speak nothing of the Indian but that which he was when this country was discovered and following. The Indian was made up of rare genius; they were capable of working material that men at this time cannot work; their whole mind was based upon the hunting of game or fighting with the white man; they were divided into different nations and tribes, which were very distinct from each other; there was a general resemblance among them, their faces being of a copper color. The language of the different nations was different, though being very much alike. They lived in huts, which they called wigwams; they were very light, and could easily be carried from one place to another. The Indian used great pride in adorning himself in gay colors. They believed in a supreme being, but not as we do. There are numbers of Indians in the west, being the descendants of the western tribes; they are kept and protected by the United State government.

LOUIS WETZEL, THE BOONE OF WEST VIRGINIA,

And His Adventures Among the Indians.

In the year of 1772 the four Zane brothers settled at the mouth of Wheeling creek; with them came an honest, brave, but rough old German, by the name of John Wetzel, the father of Louis, the bold, wary and tireless Indian hunter of West Virginia, whose name was a household word throughout the State. He was also the father of four more sons and two daughters. His sons were Martin, George, John and Jacob. The two daughters were Susan and Christina. The latter books of Indian wars which contain the story of John Wetzel, say he was killed up Wheeling creek, but the old Border Books, whose authors have talked with the notorious Louis Wetzel, say that his father was killed near Captina in 1787. "On his return from Middle Island Creek, himself and companion," says the author of the Western Border, "were in a canoe paddling slowly near the shore of the Ohio river, when they were hailed by a party of Indians, and ordered to land; this they of course refused, when immediately they were fired upon and Wetzel was shot through the body. Feeling himself mortally wounded, he directed his companion to lie down in the canoe, while he (Wetzel) so long as strength remained, would paddle the frail vessel beyond the reach of the savages; in this way he saved the life of his friend, while his own was ebbing away fast. He died soon after reaching the shore at Baker's Station, a few miles north from where he was shot." The author (McEldowney) claims that the foregoing is a true statement as to the death of John Wetzel, from the fact that a hum.

ble grave can be seen near the scene of the old fortress, and a rough stone marks the spot, bearing the inscription in rough and rude, but plain, letters:

J. W. 1787.

No man of the western border was more dreaded by an ene-my than was Louis Wetzel. By many he was regarded as nothing more than a semi-savage, a man whose disposition was that of an enraged panther, whose whole mind was upon the blood of a human being. "But it was not true," says De-haas, in his Border Wars of Western Virginia, who says: "He was never known to inflict any cruelty upon women and chil-dren, and he was never known to torture his victim as he has been charged." He had often heard his mother read these lines in the Bible: "Vengeance is mine, saith the Lord." He had received unwonted torture from the hands of the Indians; his father had been killed by them, and he was revengful for those things. When he swore to have vengeance against the whole Indian race, in the presence of his mother, brothers and Zanes at the mouth of Wheeling creek, he was joined by all of his brothers, even Jacob, who was then a mere lad, who said: "Louis, your oath is mine." He was possessed of a remarka-ble degree of intuitive knowledge, which constitutes an effi-cient hunter. He was as bold as a lion, cunning as a fox, and as quick as a squirrel. The name of Wetzel sent a thrill of horror through the breasts of the heartless savages.

The first event in the life of our hero occurred when he was but sixteen years of age. The Indians had not been very trou-blesome in the vicinity in which his father lived, and one day while he and Jacob, his younger brother, were out playing, he was amazed to find a gun pointed at him, and started to run towards the house, upon which he was shot in the breast, which wounded him severely, but not dangerously. In an in-stant two warriors sprung upon him and his brother and made them prisoners, and they were taken about twenty miles from home. During the march, Louis suffered very much with the wound he had received from their hands, but bore it with courage, knowing that if he complained he would immediately be tomahawked and scalped. When night came they built a fire and laid down to rest, but did not tie their prisoners, as was the usual custom. When the Indians were asleep, Louis having cautioned his brother in the meantime, not to sleep, they arose and pushed into the woods, where they instanly paused, Louis finding that they could go no further without moccasins; he returne to camp and secured the moccasins, and after fitting them on his brother returned to get his father's gun, which the Indians had stolen from his house, and returning, went onward till they were again among friends, having escaped from the Indians without detection.

The following are incidents in the life of Louis Wetzel, taken from the "Mirror of Olden Time Border Life."

"The first I recollect of seeing this distinguished warrior was when he attached himself to a scouting party, about the year 1787. My father then lived on the bank of the Ohio in Virginia, at a place known as the Mingo Bottom, three miles below Steubenville. A party of Indians had crossed the Ohio not far from where we lived, killed a family and then made their escape with impunity. As the Indians had not crossed the Ohio in that neighborhood, for a year or two previous the settlers began to think that they could live with safety in their cabins. This unexpected murder spread great alarm through the sparse settlement and revenge was determined upon. Some of the settlers, who were in very easy circumstances, in order to stimulate the young and active to take vengeance on the enemy, proposed to draw up a subscription, and give a handsome reward to the man who would bring the first Indian scalp. Upwards of one hundred dollars was subscribed. Major McMahon, who frequently led the hardy frontiersmen in those perilous times, soon raised a company of about twenty men, among whom was Louis Wetzel. They crossed the Ohio and pursued the Indians' trail with unerring tact, till they came to the Muskingum river. There the advance, or spies, discovered a party of Indians far superior to their own in number, camped on the bank of the river. As the Indians had not yet discov-ered the white men, Major McMahon retreated with his party to the top of the hill, where they might consult about their future operations. The conclusion of the conference was, 'that discretion was the better part of valor,' and a hasty re-treat was prudently resolved on. While the party were con-sulting on the propriety of attacking the Indians, Louis Wetzel sat on a log, with his gun laid across his lap, and his tomahawk in his hand; he took no part in the council. As soon as the resolution was adopted to retreat, it was without delay put into execution, and the party set off, leaving Louis sitting on the log. Major McMahon called to him, and inquired if he was going with them. Louis answered, "that he was not; that he came out to hunt Indians; that he was not going home like a fool with his finger in his mouth. He would take an Indian scalp, or lose his own before he went home." All their argu-ments were without avail. The stubborn, unyielding disposi-tion was such, that he never submitted himself to the control or advice of others; they were compelled to leave him, a soli-tary being in the midst of the thick forest, surrounder by vig-ilant enemies. Notwithstanding this solitary individual ap-peared to rush into danger with the fury of a mad man, in his disposition was displayed the cunning of a fox, as well as the boldness of the lion.

As soon as his friends had left him, he picked up his blanket, shouldered his rifle, and struck off into a different part of the country, in hope that fortune would place in his way some lone Indian. He kept aloof from the large streams, where large parties of the enemy generally encamped. He travelled through the woods with a noiseless tread, and the keen glance of the eagle, that day and the next, till evening, when he dis-covered a smoke curling up above the bushes. He crept softly to the fire and found two blankets and a small copper kettle in the camp. He instantly concluded that this was the camp of only two Indians, and he could kill them both. He concealed himself in the thick brush, but in such position that he could see the number and motions of the enemy. About sun set one of the Indians came in, made up the fire, and went to cooking his supper. Shortly after the other came in; they ate their suppers, after which they began to sing and amuse themselves by telling comic stories, at which they would burst into a roar of laughter. Singing and telling stories was the common practice of the white and red men when lying in their hunting camps. These poor fellows, when enjoying themselves in the utmost glee, little dreamed that the grim monster, death, in the shape of Louis Wetzel, was about stealing a march on them. Louis kept a keen watch on their maneuvers. About nine or ten o'clock at night, one of the Indians wrapped his blanket around him, shouldered his rifle, took a chunk of fire in his hands, and left the camp, doubtless with the intention of going to watch a deer lick. The fire and smoke would serve to keep off the gnats and mosquitoes. It is a remarkable fact, that deer are not alarmed at seeing fire, from the circumstance of seeing it so frequently in the fall and winter season, when the leaves and grass are dry. The absence of the Indian was the cause of vexation and disappointment to our hero, whose trap was so happily set, and he considered his game secure. He still indulged the hope that the Indians might return to camp before day. In this he was disappointed. There were birds in the woods who chirped and gave notice to the woodsman that the day would soon appear. Louis heard the wooded songsters begin to chatter, and determined to delay no longer the work of death for the return of the Indian. He walked to the camp with a noiseless step, and found his victim buried in profound sleep, lying upon his side. He drew his butcher knife, and with all his force, impelled by revenge, he thrust the blade through his heart: He said the Indian gave a short quiver and repulsive motion, and faded away in death's eternal sleep. He then scalped him, and set off for home. He arrived at Mingo Bottom only one day after his unsuccessful companions. He claimed, and as he should, received his reward.

Some time after, General Harmer had erected a fort at the mouth of Muskingum river. He prevailed upon some white men to go with a flag among the nearest Indian tribes, and endeavor to prevail with them to come to the fort, and there to conclude a treaty of peace. A large number of Indians came on general invitation, and camped on the Muskingum river, a few miles above its mouth. General Harmer issued a proclamation, giving notice that a cessation of arms was mutually agreed upon, between the white and the red men, till an effort for a treaty of peace was made. As treaties of peace with the Indians had been so frequently violated, but little faith was placed in the stability of such treaties by the frontiersmen, notwithstanding they were as frequently the aggressors, as were the Indians. Half of the frontier men of that day had been born in a fort and grew to manhood, as it were, in a siege. The Indian war had continued so long and was so bloody that they believed war with them was to continue as long as one lived to make fight. With these oppressions, as they considered the Indian truthless, it was difficult to inspire confidence in the stability of such treaties. While General Harmer was diligently engaged in making peace with the Indians, Wetzel concluded to go to Fort Harmer, and as the Indians would be passing and repassing between their camp and the Fort, would offer a fair opportunity for killing one. He associated himself in this enterprise with Veich Dick.inson, who was only a small grade below himself in restless. ness and daring. As soon as the enterprise was resolved upon, the desired point, and set themselves down in ambush near the

path leading from the fort and the Indian camp. Shortly after they had concealed themselves by the wayside, they saw an
Indian approaching on horse-back, running his horse at full
speed. They called to him, but owing to the clatter of the
horse's feet, he did not heed or hear their call, but kept on at
a sweeping gallop. When the Indian had nearly passed they
concluded to give him a fire as he rode. They fired, but as the
Indian did not fall they thought they had missed him. As the
alarm would soon be spread that an Indian had been shot at,
and as large numbers of them were at hand, they commenced
an immediate retreat to their home. As their neighbors well
knew their object, as soon as they returned they were asked
what luck. Wetzel answered that they had bad luck; that
they shot at an Indian on horseback and missed him; but the
truth was, that they had shot him in the lower part of his body
on which he rode to camp, and expired that night of his wound.

It was soon rumored that Lewis Wetzel was the murderer.
General Harmer sent a Captain Kingsbury with a company of
men to the Mingo Bottom, with orders to take Wetzel, dead or
alive, a useless and impotent order. A company of men could
as easily have taken Old Horny out of the bottomless pit as
to take Lewis Wetzel by force from the neighborhood of Mingo
Bottom. On the day Captain Kingsbury arrived, there was a
shooting match at my father's, and Lewis was there. As soon
as the object of Captain Kingsbury was ascertained, it was resolved to ambush the Captain's barge and kill him and his
men. Happily, Major McMahon was present to prevent this
catastrophe, and prevailed upon Wetzel and his friends to suspend the attack until he could pay Captain Kingsbury a visit,
and perhaps he would prevail with them to return without
making an attempt to take Wetzel. With a great deal of reluctance they agreed to suspend the attack until Major McMahon returned. The resentment and fury of Wetzel and his
men were boiling and blowing like the steam from a steamboat. "A pretty affair is this," they said, "to hang a man for

killing an Indian, when they are killing some of our people
every day." Major McMahon informed Captain Kingsbury of
the force and fury of the people, and assured them if they per-
sisted in the attempt to seize Wetzel that he would have all
of the settlers in the country upon him; that nothing could
save them from being massacred, but a speedy return. The
Captain took his advice and forthwith returned to Fort Harmer. Wetzel now considered the affair as finally settled. As
Lewis was never long stationary, but ranged at will along the
river from Ft. Pitt to the falls of the Ohio, and was a welcome
guest and perfectly at home wherever he went, shortly after
the attempt to seize him by Captain Kingsbury and his men,
he got into a canoe with the intention of proceeding down the
Ohio river to Kentucky. He had a friend by the name of
Hamilton Carr, who had lately settled on an island near Ft.
Harmer. Here he stopped, with the intention of stopping for
the night. By some means, which never was explained, General Harmer was advised of his being on the island. A guard
was sent who crossed to the island, surrounded Mr. Carr's
house, went in, and as Wetzel lay asleep he was seized by numbers, his hands and feet were securely bound, and he was hur-
ried to a boat, and from thence placed in a guard room, where
he was loaded with irons. The ignominy of wearing iron hand
cuffs and hobbles, and being chained down, to a man of his independent and resolute spirit was more than he could bear; it
was to him more painful than death; shortly after he was con.
fined, he sent for General Harmer, and requested a visit. The
General went. Wetzel admitted without hesitation, "that he
had shot an Indian." As he did not wish to be hung like a
dog, he requested the General to give him up to the Indians,
as there was a large number present. "He might place them
all in a circle, with their scalping knives and tomahawks, and
give him a tomahawk, and place him in the midst of the circle,
and then let him and the Indians fight it out in the best way
they could." The General told him, "That he was an officer

appointed by the law, by which he must be governed. As the
law did not authorize him to make such a compromise, he
could not grant his request." After a few days longer confinement, he again sent for the General to come and see him;
and he did so. Wetzel said, he "had never been confined, and
could not live much longer if he was not permitted to walk
about." The General ordered the officer on guard to knock off
his iron fetters but to leave on his handcuffs, and permit him
to walk about on the point at the mouth of the Muskingum;
but to be sure and keep a close watch upon him. As soon as
they were outside of the fort gate, Lewis began to caper about
like a wild colt broke loose from the stall. He would start
and run a few yards as if he was about making an escape, then
turn round and join the guard. The next start he would run
farther, and then stop. In this way he amused the guard for
some time, at every start running a little farther. At length,
he called forth all his strength, resolution and activity, and determined on freedom or an early grave. He gave a sudden
spring forward, and bounded off at the top of his speed for the
shelter of his beloved woods. His movement was so quick,
and so unexpected, that the guard were taken by surprise, and
he got nearly a hundred yards before they recovered their as-
tonishment. They fired, but all missed; they followed in pursuit, but he soon left them out of sight. As he was well acquainted with the country, he made for a dense thicket, two
or three miles from the fort. In the midst of this thicket he
found a tree which had fallen across a log, where the brush
were very close. Under the tree he squeezed his body. The
brush were so thick that he could not be discovered unless his
pursuers examined very closely. As soon as his escape was
announced, General Harmer started the soldiers and Indians
in pursuit. After he had laid about two hours in his place of
concealment, two Indians came into the thicket and stood on
the log, under which he lay concealed. His heart beat so vio-
lently he was afraid they would hear it thumping. He could

hear them hallooing in every direction, as they hunted through the brush. At length, the evening wore away the day, he found himself alone in the friendly thicket. But what could he do? His hands were fastened with iron cuffs and bolts, and he knew of no friend on the same side of the Ohio to whom he could apply for assistance. He had a friend who had recently put up a cabin on the Virginia side of the Ohio, who, he had no doubt, would lend him any assistance in his power. With the most gloomy foreboding of the future, a little after night-fall he left the thicket and made his way to the Ohio. He came to the river about three or four miles below the fort. He took this circuit, as he expected guards would be set at every point where he could find a canoe. How to get across the river was the all-important question. He could not make a raft with his hands bound. He was an excellent swimmer, but he was fearful he could not swim the Ohio with his heavy iron handcuffs. After pausing some time, he determined to make the attempt. Nothing worse than death could happen; and he would prefer drowning to again falling into the hands of Harmer and his Indians. Like the illustrious Caesar in the storm, he would trust the event to fortune; and he plunged into the river. He swam the greatest part of the distance on his back, and reached the Virginia shore in safety; but so much exhausted that he had to lay on the beach some time before he was able to rise. He went to the cabin of his friend, where he was received with rapture. A file and hammer soon released him from his iron handcuffs. His friend (I have forgotten his name) furnished him with a gun, ammunition and blanket, and he was again free, and prepared to engage in any new enterprise that would strike his fancy. He got into a canoe, and went to Kentucky, where he considered himself safe fram the grasp of General Harmer.

After this unfortunate happening he went south, where he staid for about five years, and his friends and relatives were wondering as to his whereabouts, and upon inquiry learned of his close confinement at Natches, having been convicted of a felony; some say counterfeiting, and some say being intimate with the wife of a Spaniard; the latter probably being the cause. His friends immediately received a pardon for him, upon which he returned home (Wheeling), where he resided with a near relative, Mrs. George Crookis, and upon being joked by her, she asked him if it was not about time for him to choose a wife, upon which he replied that "there is no one in this world for him, but in Heaven." He returned south after being at the Crookis homestead for a number of years, vowing to avenge himself against the Spaniard, who had put him in jail for something he said he had never done. Whether he did or not was never known. "The appearance of Louis Wetzel," says Judge Foster, "looked to be about twenty-six years of age, about five feet ten inches high, being full breasted and very broad across the shoulders, his face being heavily pitted from the effects of smallpox; his hair reached to the calves of his legs." David McIntire, of the county of Belmont, Ohio, was the last man known to have seen Louis Wetzel. He saw him at Natches, where he was on a visit to a friend, one Phillip Sykes. He died in 1808. The number of scalps taken by him is unestimable; the best authorities estimate it at something near one hundred.

STOUT HEARTED LOUIS WETZEL.

Stout hearted Louis Wetzel
  Rides down the river shore,
The wilderness behind him,
  The wilderness before.

He rides in the cool of morning,
  Humming the dear old tune,
"Into the heart of the greenwood,
  Into the heart of June."

He needs no guide in the forest
  More than the honey bees;
His guides are the cool green mosses
  To the northward of the trees.

Nor fears him the foe whose footstep
  Is light as the summer air;
His tomahawk hangs in his shirt belt,
  The scalp knife glitters there.

The stealthy Wyandottes tremble
  And speak his name with fear,
For his aim is sharp and deadly,
  And his rifle's ring is clear.

So pleasantly rides he onward,
  Pausing to hear the stroke
Of the settler's ax in the forest,
  Or the crack of a falling oak.

The partridge drums on the dry oak,
  The croaking croby crows,
The black bird sings in the spice bush,
  The robin in the haws.

And as they chatter and twitter,
  The wild bird seems to say:
"Do not harm us, good Louis,
  And you shall have luck to-day."

A sharp clear ring through the greenwood,
  And with mightier leap and bound,
The pride of the western forest
  Lies bleeding on the ground.

Then out from the leafy shadows
  A stalwart hunter springs,
And his unsheathed scalp knife glittering,
  Against his rifle rings.

"And who art thou," quoth Louis,
  "That comest twixt me and mine?"
And his cheek is flushed with anger,
  As a bacchant's flushed with wine.

"What boots that to thy purpose?"
  The stranger hot replies;
"My rifle marked it living,
  And mine, when dead, the prize."

Then with sinewy arms they grapple,
  Like giants fierce in brawls,
Till stretched along greensward
  The humble hunter falls.

"Now take this rod of alder,
  Set it by yonder tree
A hundred yards beyond me,
  And wait you there and see."

"For he who dares such peril
  But lightly holds his breath,
May his unshrieved soul be ready
  To welcome sudden death."

So the stranger takes the alder,
  And wandering stands in view,
While Wetzel's aim grows steady
  And he cuts the rod in two.

"By heavens," exclaims the stranger,
  "One only, far and nigh,
Hath arms like the lithe young ash tree
  Or half so keen an eye,"

"And that is Louis Wetzel,"
  Quoth Louis. "Here he stands."
So they speak in gentle manner
  And clasp their friendly hands.

Ride out of the leafy greenwood,
  As rises the yellow moon,
And the purple hills lie pleasantly
  In the softened air of June.

                        —FLOHUS B. PIMPTON.

SIMON GIRTY.

The notorious Simon Girty once led a band of savages through Wetzel county. We here give a sketch of him, taken from McDonald's History of Ohio.

Simon Girty was from Pennsylvania, to which his father had emigrated from Ireland. The old man was beastly intemperate, and nothing ranked higher in his estimation than a jug of whisky. Grog was his song, and grog he would have. His sottishness turned his wife's affection. Ready for seduction, she yielded her heart to a neighboring rustic, who, to remove all obstacles to their wishes, knocked Girty on the head and bore off the trophy of his prowess. Four sons of this interesting couple were left, Thomas, Simon, George and James. The three latter were taken prisoners in Braddock's war by the Indians. George was adopted by the Delawares, became a ferocious savage, and died in a drunken fit. James was adopted by the Swanees, and became as depraved as his other brothers. It is said that he often visited Kentucky at the time of its first settlement, and inflicted most barbarous tortures upon all captive women who came within his reach. Traders who were acquainted with him say so ferocious was he that he would not have turned on his heel to save a prisoner from the flames. To this monster are to be attributed many of the cruelties charged upon his brother Simon, yet he was caressed by Proctor and Elliott. Simon was adopted by the Senecas, and became an expert hunter; in Kentucky and Ohio he sustained the character of an unrelenting barbarian. One hundred years ago his name was associated with everything that was cruel and fiendlike; to the women and children particularly, nothing was more terrifying than the name of Simon

Girty.   At that time it was believed by many that he had fled
from justice and was seeking refuge among the Indians, determined to do his countrymen all the harm in his power.   This
impression was as erroneous one; being adopted by the Indians, he joined them in their wars and conformed to their
usages.   This was the education he had received, and their foes
were his.   Although trained in all his pursuits as an Indian, it
is said to be a fact susceptible of proof that through his importance many prisoners were saved from death.   His influence was great, and when he chose to be merciful it was generally in his power to protect the imploring captive.   His reputation was that of an honest man, and be fulfilled his engage-
ments to the last cent.   It is said he once sold his horse, rather
than to incur the odium of violating his promise.   He was intemperate, and when intoxicated ferocious and abusive to
friends.   Although much disabled the last ten years of his life
by rheumatism, he rode to his hunting ground in pursuit of
game, suffering the most excruciating pains.   He often boasted of his warlike spirit.   It was his constant wish, one that
was gratified, that he might die in battle.   He was at Proctor's
defeat, and cut to pieces by Colonel Johnson's men.   Girty led
the first attack against Fort Henry in 1777; he also led an attack against Baker's fort the same year, but without effect.

FORT HENRY, AT WHEELING, W. VA.

Wetzel county was at one time a part of Ohio county, and was during the sieges of Fort Henry, and a sketch of the sieges would be appropriate. We have selected a sketch written by G. L. Cranmer.

Originally called Fort Fincastle in honor of Lord Dunmore, who, at the time of its erection, was Governor of the Colony, in the year 1776 its name was changed to Fort Henry, in honor of Patrick Henry, the first Governor of the Commonwealth. It was erected in the year 1774, the immediate cause of its erection being found in the fact that an apprehended attack from the savages during that year was anticipated, and a place of defence for the protection of the infant settlement, of which they were destitute, was demanded. It was planned by General Gorge Rogers Clark, Commandant of the Western Military Department, and was built by the settlers.

In shape it was a parallelogram, being about three hundred and fifty-six feet in length and about one hundred and fifty feet in width, and was surrounded by pickets about twelve feet high with bastions at each corner. Inside of the stockade cabins were erected for the shelter of such as sought protection, a magazine for military stores, a block house, the second story of which projected over the lower, filled with port holes, through which the trusty rifle of the pioneer sent its death-dealing missile. On the top of the block house was a mounted swivel, a four pounder, which did effective work in an emergency. Wells were also sunk in the inclosure, so that a supply of water was secured at all times.

To the southeast, and about fifty yards distant from the Fort, stood the residence of Col. Ebenezer Zane—a cabin built of rough-hewn logs, with a kitchen or outbuilding in the rear, which also had attached to it a magazine for military stores.

This house served as an outpost during the last siege of the Fort, which occurred on the 11th day of September, 1782, and contributed greatly to the defeat of the Indians and their British allies on that memorable occasion. There were two regular sieges of the Fort—the one in the year 1777 and the other in the year 1782, both of which were successfully repulsed. At the last siege the Indians were commanded by James Girty, and the British troops by Captain Pratt. Many writers name Simon Girty as the one in command on this occasion, but this is a mistake, as at this time he was with an Indian army which had invaded the territory of Kentucky, and he was present with that force at its attack on Bryant's Station, which occurred but a short time prior to the attack on Fort Henry.

James Girty was even more vindictive and bloodthirsty than his brother Simon Girty, but was not so conspicuous a character as the latter. There is reason to believe, however, that many of the atrocious deeds attributed to Simon Girty, the recital of which even at this late date makes the blood to run cold with horror, were perpetrated by James.

On the happening of the last siege the settlers on short and sudden notice had barely time to escape to the shelter of the Fort, so unexpected was the appearance of the savages. Consequently their homes, together with their furniture, were left exposed to the rapacity and cupidity of their assailants. It was towards evening that the Indian force with their allies appeared, and from that time until midnight repeated and furious assaults were made by them on the Fort and its inmates, which were as often repulsed.

Awaiting the dawn of day, the attacks were renewed, but with as little success as during the preceding night. In the afternoon of the second day the besieged, finding their stock of powder had almost given out, it became with them a serious question as to how they were to obtain a supply. There was plenty of it in the magazine at the house of Col. Zane, but apparently for all practical purposes it might have been a hundred miles distant. In this juncture Silas Zane, who was in command of the Fort, called atention to the critical state of affairs, and asked for volunteers to undertake the perilous feat of going to Col. Zane's house for the purpose of obtaining the needed supply. Several young men fleet of foot as well as bold and intrepid, offered their services, and each clamored to have the preference in an enterprise which, humanly speaking, boded almost certain death.

At this crisis a young lady seventeen years of age, who had been engaged in moulding bullets and loading the guns of the men during the siege, stepped forward and besought her brother, Silas Zane, to permit her to undertake the arduous task, accompanying her arguments with representations to the effect that she, being a woman, could be more easily spared than a man; that each man was needed for the defence, and that the loss of her life as compared with one of the sterner sex would be a small matter. Her arguments prevailed and she was permitted to essay the effort.

Divesting herself of superfluous clothing, the gates were thrown open for her egress, when, bounding forth with the fleetness of a deer, her long black hair streaming like a banner on the air, she rapidly sped in the direction of her brother's house, which she reached in security. Not a rifle had been raised nor a shot fired at her, the Indians, when they saw her, contemptuously exclaiming, "A squaw," "A squaw."

Hastily communicating her errand, Col. Zane snatched a table-cloth at hand, which he securely bound around her waist, and emptying into it the coveted powder, she set out on her return. She had covered about half the distance between the house and the Fort, when the savages, apprehending her purpose, fired a storm of bullets at her person, which happily proved harmless. In recounting her adventures subsequently, and especially this stirring incident, she would relate that the bullets whistled around her so thick and came so fast that her eyes were blinded with the dust so that she could scarcely distinguish her way to the fort. As the gates were thrown open for her entrance, the Indians made an unavailing effort to reach them by rushing towards them and securing an ingress.

This act of heroism upon the part of Elizabeth Zane saved the lives of the inmates of the Fort and enabled them to successfully withstand the siege.

In the meantime the besiegers had been greatly harrassed and embarrassed by the continual firing from Col. Zane's house, which as an outpost contributed largely to the protection of the stockade. On the second night it was therefore resolved by the Indians to attempt its destruction. About midnight the savages became quiet and they had suffered their fires to die out, while a hush of silence rested on the scene around. The vigilance of the occupants of the house, however, was not deceived by appearances.

Old Sam, a Guinea negro who belonged to and was strongly attached to his master, Col. Zane, was on the alert with his trusty rifle in hand. He perceived a dark object with a lighted brand wriggling along on the ground, which ever and anon would wave to and fro in the air and blow upon it to rekindle. Allowing the Indian, for such it was, to approach within sure range, Sam fired, when the savage jumped to his feet, but fell back again yelling with rage and pain, until he either made his own way off or was aided to do so by others. Twice during the night did Sam frustrate two similar attempts on the part of the Indians.

Old Sam and his wife were cared for assiduously until their death. They lived for many years after in a cabin which was erected for them on the upper portion of the Island, and died in peace and contentment, honored and respected by all who knew them, whose name was legion.

On the morning of the third day the Indians held a pow-wow or council and determined to raise the siege, greatly to the relief of the inmates of the house and Fort. With demonstrations of disgust and contempt they turned their backs upon the besieged, the greater portion of them recrossing the river, while a smaller portion went on a raid against some of the smaller forts back of Wheeling in the vicinity of the Pennsylvania line.

While peace between Great Britain and the Colonies had not yet been proclaimed, and was not for some months subsequent, yet virtually it did prevail and continued until its formal declaration, so that this siege of Fort Henry was the last battle of the Revolution, and the capstone of the war was laid on the soil of Western Virginia.

Elizabeth Zane, the heroine of Fort Henry, was twice married—the first time to a man by the name of Clark, and all her life was spent in the immediate vicinity of the scene of her exploits. Her immediate descendants have all deceased, but her heroism will ever remain as a monument to perpetuate her name and fame.

Unless speedily rescued, the past with all its splendid achievements, its incidents and its memories, will be swallowed up in oblivion. To the youth of our land we therefore appeal not to let these things die. Let them become the guardians of our pioneer history, and by frequent recurrence to the scenes of the past restore their loyalty and revive their patriotism.

DAVID MORGAN'S ADVENTURE.

In the neighborhood of what was once Prickett's Fort, Monangalia county, then Virginia, a sanguinary contest took place between Capt. David Morgan and two Indians. Morgan was at that time over sixty years of age. In the early part of April, feeling himself unwell, he sent his two children, Stephen, a youth of sixteen, and Sara, a girl of fourteen, to feed the cattle at his farm, about a mile off. The children, thinking to remain all day, and spend the time in preparing ground to plant watermelons, unknown to their father took with them some bread and meat. Having fed the stock, Stephen set himself to work, and while he was engaged in grubbing his sister would remove the brush, and otherwise aid him in the labor of clearing the ground, occasionally going to the house to wet some linen which she had spread out to bleach. Morgan, after the children had been gone some time, betook himself to bed, and soon falling asleep, dreamed that he saw Stephen and Sara walking about the fortyard, scalped. Aroused from slumber by the harrowing spectacle presented to his sleeping view, he inquired if the children had returned, and was informed that they had not. He then set out to see what detained them, taking with him his gun. As he approached the house, still impressed with the horrible fear that he should find his dream true, he ascended an eminence from which he could distinctly see over his plantation, and descrying from thence the objects of his anxious solicitude, he went near where the children were working, and seated himself on a log. He had been there but a few minutes, when he saw two Indians come out from the house and start toward the children, on which he told them in a careful manner to make for the fort at once, as they were in great danger. They started to run and the Indians took after them, but the old gentleman showing himself at this instant, caused them to forbear the chase and shelter themselves behind treees. The old man then tried to escape by flight, and the Indians took after him. His age and his health prevented him from keeping out of their reach, and finding that they were gaining on him, he turned around to shoot, on which the savages took shelter behind trees, Morgan doing the same thing. The one that the Indian got behind was too small to shelter him, and Morgan seeing that a part of his body was in view, shot and killed him. Having succeeded in killing one of the savages he again took to flight, and the remaining Indian again took after him. The race continued for about sixty yards; Morgan was fast giving out. He looked over his shoulder and saw the Indian not ten steps behind him, with his gun raised as if he was going to fire. Morgan then dodged to one side and the bullet went whizzing past him. The odds now were not so great as before, and Morgan stopped running and made at the savage with his gun, on which the Indian hurled a tomahawk at him, cutting two of his fingers off and injuring another severely. They then grabbed holds, and Morgan, being a good wrestler, threw his adversary, but found himself turned. The savage was now on top of him, feeling for his knife and sending forth a most terrific yell, as is their custom when thinking a victory secure. A woman's apron, which the Indian had taken from the house and fastened around him above his knife, hindered him from getting at it quickly, and Morgan, getting one of his fingers in his mouth, deprived him of the use of one hand. The Indian at last got hold of his knife, catching it on the lower part of the blade. Morgan, too, got a small hold on the extremity of the handle, and as the Indian drew it from the scabbard Morgan bit his finger so hard that he relaxed his hold, thus giving Morgan a chance to draw it through his hand, cutting it severely. By this time both had

gained their feet, and the savage, seeing the advantage that
Morgan was gaining over him. tried to disengage himself, but
Morgan held fast to him and succeeded in giving him a fatal
blow that made the almost lifeless body sink in his arms. He
then loosened his hold and departed for the fort. On his way
he met his daughter, who not being able to keep pace with her
brother, was following his footsteps. Assured thus far of the
safety of his children, he accompanied his daughter to the fort
and then returned with a company of men to see if there were
any more Indians about. On arriving at the spot where the
battle took place, the wounded Indian was not to be seen, but
they trailed him by the blood to the branches of a fallen tree,
and as they approached him he saluted them familiarly: "How
do do, broder; how do do, broder." Alas, poor fellow, but
their brotherhood extended no farther than to the gratification
of a vengeful feeling. He was tomahawked and scalped. He
and his companion were flayed, their skins tanned and converted into saddle seats, shot pouches and belts. On the day of the
unveiling of the monument that was erected in his memory on
the site of the combat in Monongalia county, there was on ex-
hibition at the spot a shot pouch and saddle girth made from
the skins of the same Indians he killed. The shot pouch is now
in the possession of ——————, of this county. The knife
that the Indians were killed with is owned by some of Morgan's descendants in Marion county.

LEVI MORGAN.

The people of Wetzel county are interested in the life and deeds of Levi Morgan, from the fact that Hon. Aaron Morgan, at the recent session of the Legislature, obtained an appropriation from that body of $3,500, for the erection of a monument in the court house yard at New Martinsville in his honor. The author has used great pains in securing the deeds of him more than anything else, his place of birth, for the year is not known by the author, and is unable to find out, neither can he obtain the year of his death. All that we can find out is that he moved on a farm near Louisville, Kentucky, after Wayne's treaty. In 1878 the Indians visited the settlement on Buffalo, in Pennsylvania, and Levi Morgan was there, skinning a wolf, which he had just taken from a trap. He saw three Indians, one riding a horse which belonged to a neighbor of his, and one that he knew very well, having rode it number of times previous. The other two were walking close behind, coming toward him. On looking in the direction they were coming, he recognized the horse and supposed the rider to be its owner, and on looking again discovered his mistake, and quickly seized his gun, sprang behind a large boulder, the Indians taking shelter behind trees as soon as he was from their view. He turned and glanced around the rock and found that the Indians were looking for him at the other end of the rock, and seeing one peep out, immediately pulled his gun and fired, on which the Indian fell dead. But on turning to reload his gun, found that he had left his powder horn where he was skinning the wolf. He then darted from behind the rock with all of his speed, and one of the savages took after him. For some time he held his own in the race, but the savage, being used to such

work, began to gain on him.   The chances were very slim now
for Morgan, and seeing this he threw his gun down, thinking
that the Indian would be amazed at the idea, and pick up the
gun, but the Indian did nothing of the kind and passed by it
as though it had never been dropped.   He then threw his shot
pouch and coat in the way, but his schemes were in vain.
They ran on until they reached the top of the hill.   Here he
stopped, and as though some one was on the other side of the
hill, called out: "Come on, come on; here's one, make haste."
The Indian, thinking that he was calling upon some one on the
other side of the hill, immediately beat a hasty retreat.   Morgan then exclaimed: "Shoot quick, or he will be out of reach."
The Indian seemed to double the thought, and hastened his
speed.   Morgan then turned and went home, being pleased
with his success, leaving his gun, shot pouch and coat to reward the savage for the deception practiced upon him.

At the treaty of Augliaxe he met the Indian who had given
him such a chase, and he still had the gun that Morgan had
thrown down.   After talking over the circumstance, they decided to test the ownership of it by a friendly race.   The Indian being beaten, rubbed his hands and said: "Stiff, stiff; too
old, too old."   "Well," said Morgan, "you got the gun by outrunning me then, and I should have it for outrunning you
now," and accordingly took it.

In the year of 1790 Levi Morgan was made captain of a
company of nineteen men who were stationed at the mouth of
Big Fishing creek, where he had erected a fort.   They built
two sixty-foot canoes and descended downward on their way to
the mouth of the Muskingum, where they were going to attack
an Indian camp seven miles up the river.   When they arrived
at the desired point they hid their canoes in the bushes and stationed two men to watch them until they returned, and if they
did not return in three days to make their way as fast as possible to the fort.   Captain Morgan, with the remaining seven-

teen men, struck cautiously through the woods westward and traveled several miles, until they struck a large cove at the head of a stream which ran into the Ohio. They heard a bell jingle at the head of the cove, on which Morgan exclaimed: "Boys, get your guns ready and see that your powder is handy." He had a boy in his company who was but sixteen years of age. His name was Hays (see the story of the two half Indians.) He put his men in two's taking the boy with him, and gave or-ders that when the first gun was fired that they were to run into the camp with a knife in one hand and a gun in another. One was to run around one way and one another, and run the Indians out of their wigwams, if possible, without their guns, and if not, to shoot the first Indian seen with a gun. Morgan and Hays were the first ones to see the Indians, who saw one salting some ponies. Morgan said to Hays: "I will split that Indian's nose, right between his eyes," on which he shot and killed the Indian. They then raised a yell and rushed into camp and found no one there but a few Indian squaws and some young men. There were about five hundred wigwams in the village and about six hundred bushels of corn. One of the old Indian squaws asked Morgan if they had killed a young In-dian, and he told her they had not, and she said there was one missing. They then knew that one had gotten away. After catching all the horses they needed, they burned the village and told the old Indian squaw that they wanted to go to the Muskingum river, and if she would take them there that they would not harm her, but if she didn't, they would kill all of them. She took them straight through, traveling both night and day, until they reached the place where they had hid their canoes. It was the fourth day, but the men were still there. They then tied the two canoes together and put the ponies into them, putting the hind feet in one and the front feet in the other. A couple of men rowed the boats to the mouth of the Muskingum, and after crossing over to the Virginia side they sank the boats and went by land to Pricket's Fort, in Monongalia county. They kept the prisoners until Wayne's treaty, when they were given up, and it was at that place that the Drygoo boys were obtained. Morgan was at the defeat of St. Clair and shot at the white renegade, Simon Girty.

OUR EARLY SETTLER.

The earliest white settler along the Ohio river, in Wetzel county, was Edward Doolin, who came here about the year 1780, and made a settlement near Doolin's spring, one mile from the mouth of Fishing creek, on lands now owned by the heirs of Phillip Witten. He there built two cabins, one for himself and wife and the other for his negro slave. He owned a large survey of lands lying on both sides of the stream which still bears his name; lines of his survey are well established, and have been familiar to the courts of Wetzel in divers suits of ejectments.

He had hardly broken the solitude of the vast wilderness, when he was visited by a tribe of Delaware Indians, who came at night and took away his negro slave into captivity, and returning at daybreak, and finding Doolin in his front door yard, shot and scalped him. His wife, who was still in the cabin lying abed with a newborn babe beside her, was not molested. Mrs. Doolin was a woman of remarkable beauty, and the savages, fearing it might prove fatal to compel her to accompany them while in her delicate state of health, urged her to remain there for a few days, until she entirely recovered, promising to rturn and take her with them to be the wife of their great chief. This alluring prospect, however, did not seem to have charmed the white beauty into lingering there.

At that time a blockhouse stood near the present residence of Mrs. Eliza Martin, in the limits of the present town of New Martinsville. Its solitary inmate, when these occurrences took place, was a man named Martin, who heard the report of the firing in the early morning, in the direction of Doolin's clearing. He made a reconnaissance and found the body of Doolin

lying in front of his cabin. Entering the house he wrapped
Mrs. Doolin in blankets and, taking the infant in his arms, assisted her to the blockhouse, where he placed the widow and
orphan in a canoe and transported them up the Ohio to the
mouth of Captina creek. He then returned with comrades,
and they buried the body of Doolin in the spot known as Witten's garden, where his grave is still to be seen. And every
spring the Easter flowers bloomed over the dust of Edward
Doolin—the first white settler of Wetzel, and one of the few
white men killed by the Indians within her borders.

Mrs. Doolin lived near the settlement until her daughter had
grown to be a girl of ten.   She then married and went to Kentucky, where her daughter, after she had grown to be a young
lady, married one Daniel Boone, a descendant of the noted Indian scout, Daniel Boone.   Mrs. Doolin sold this land to the
Martins, McEldowneys and Wittens, and from her or her ancestors have never been heard of since.

MORGAN MORGAN.

Morgan Morgan was commonly known as Spymod. It was to distinguish him from his cousin, Morgan Morgan, who was known as Paddymod. The former came to what is now Pine Grove in 1805, and erected a mill on the ground now occupied by Hennen's livery barn; he also owned land where Reader now stands.

We give here the following incidents in the life of Morgan: While he was at Morgantown, or what is now known as that place, he went on a spying expedition, and it was from that he got the nickname of Spymod. The expedition wandered into what is now known as the "Jug," on Middle Island creek, and above the first run Morgan shot a turkey. They then left a man at the mouth of the first run as a guard, and told him not to shoot unless it was at an Indian. The other members of the crowd, including Morgan, went up the run a short distance to cook the turkey Morgan had just shot, and just as they got the turkey ready to cook they heard a shot in the direction one of their men was stationed, on which they dropped the turkey, picked up their guns and made in the direction of the firing. On reaching there they found that he had shot a wolf, which was done by compulsion. The wolf had come toward him and he had tried to scare it away, but in vain. The wolf kept coming toward him and was six inches from the muzzle of his gun when he shot.

The creek makes a small bend above the "Jug," and while talking the matter over about the killing of the wolf they saw two Indians dart out from behind trees and run down the creek. Morgan took after them, but was stopped by two of his companions who told him that there was liable to be a band

somewhere near that neighborhood, and they supposed the Indians were sent out to see what the first firing was. They then
followed the Indian trail to the "Jug," which was but a short
distance, and it was found that the two Indians had gone
around the "Jug," on which it was decided that it would be
best for them to go through the "Jug." On arriving at the
head of it, they found that a band of Indians had been there
but a short time previous. It was then decided to make for
the fort, which was situated at New Martinsville and owned
by Morgan's brother, Levi Morgan.

Another incident in his life worthy of mention is one of his
narrow escapes on one of his spying expeditions. Himself and
another man were appointed to spy around the old Indian trail
from Morgantown to the mouth of Big Fishing creek, to see if
there were Indians about. On one occasion his pardner was
sick and it was prevailed on him to go alone. He started one
rainy day and before he stopped he had reached what is now
Pine Grove. It was still raining, the rain pouring down in torrents, and wishing to strike a dry spot, crawled into a hollow
sycamore tree, which was known by him and his pardner on
their expeditons as a resting place. It was getting about dusk;
he had been there but a few minutes when an Indian came
running to the tree and looked inside. Morgan seeing this,
drew his butcher knife ready for action, but he did not use it,
the hole being so dark the Indian could see nothing, and turned
and darted onward at the same speed he had come up. This
aroused Morgan's suspicion, and he immediately began to hunt
for new quarters, going direct to the mouth of Big Fishing
creek.

THE STORY OF CROW'S RUN.

In the early spring of 1782, a squad of men started out from Fort Henry on a hunting expedition. Among them was a man by the name of Crow, of whom our story relates. They traveled onward until they reached the mouth of what is now Big Fishing creek, which empties into the Ohio at New Martinsville. They followed the creek until they reached the mouth of a run putting into Big Fishing creek, twelve miles from New Martinsville. Here they camped on the east side of the creek on the ground now owned by John Lantz. After camping for the night, the next day they went in search of game, which was then plentiful in that neighborhood, with three men in one company and two in another, Crow being in the company of two. After hunting all day, at sunset the two came toward camp carrying the game they had shot, and on reaching the camp Crow's companion started out to get some wood to build a fire to cook a part of the game they had shot, and was hardly gone when a band of Indians surrounded the camp, and Crow, realizing that he was menaced by a terrible danger, started to run, on which a volley of shots were poured upon him, and one hit him in the head and killed him instantly. His companion on hearing the shots, started toward camp, and seeing the Indians began to run as Crow did, but was not so unfortunate, though shot in the hip, which did not hinder him from running on until he reached the company of three, who were running toward the camp in full speed, having heard the shots that were fired at Crow, and suspicioned that which was correct. The Indians, on the other hand, thinking that a superior force of men were somewhere in the neighborhood, immediately re-treated. The remaining members of the company returned to

camp, and found Crow lying dead near the creek with his head
partially in the water.   They picked him up and placed him in
a hollow sycamore tree and covered him up to keep the wolves
from carrying the body off until they returned to the fort to secure reinforcements, and bury him.   They went to Wheeling
and secured the reinforcements and returned in four days and
buried him under a sycamore tree, using walnut logs for his
coffin, and inscribed on the tree, "J. J. Crow, 1782."   The tree
stood until about the vear of 1875, when it was blown down by
the wind, and it was from this unfortunate being that the name
of Crow's run was obtained.

THE DRYGOOS, OR THE TWO HALF INDIANS.

John Hays came to what is known as Lot in the year of 1805 and with him he brought his wife, Mrs. Elizabeth Hays, who was born the same day as her husband, which was in the year of 1748, in Pricket's Fort, Monongalia county. They were but eleven years old when the latter's mother, Mrs. Drygoo, was killed by the Indians.

The following is an incident which fell from the lips of Mrs. Hays, told to her daughter, Mrs. Malinda Anderson: It was in a fort situated on Clinton's run, Monongalia county, known as Prickett's fort. The Drygoo family were some of its occupants. There was a garden about half a mile from the fort, and Mrs. Drygoo and her son, Charles, who was but four years of age, went to the garden to pick beans, when the Indians came upon them unawares and made them prisoners before giving them time to call for help. They tied Mrs. Drygoo to a tree near the fort, but not in sight, and returned to the garden to see if they could catch some more in the same way. In a little while Mrs. Hays and her sister came out of the fort and started toward the garden to help their mother (Mrs. Drygoo) pick beans, and as they neared the garden started to call for their mother, but she did not answer. Fortunately they got scared at something (not the Indians) and started toward the fort at full speed, and on reaching it informed the occupants that their mother, Mrs. Drygoo, and their brother, Charles Dry. goo, started out in the garden some time ago to pick beans and that they were not in the garden now. The men immediately suspicioned that which was correct and soon raised a company

under Captain David Morgan and went in pursuit. The Indians, seeing that they had been discovered, beat a hasty retreat. They untied Mrs. Drygoo and put her on a pony, which
was very wild, and made off with great speed. After traveling
for about ten miles the pony she was on jumped a run. The
calf of one of her legs was torn open, having caught on a sharp
limb of a tree. They stopped and bandaged the wound up the
best way they could, after which they continued their journey,
but the bandage did no good, and she became very weak from
loss of blood. The Indians, seeing that it was delaying their
journey, decided to kill her. When they began to untie her
from the pony Charles began to cry and a big Indian picked
him up and said "Don't cry," that they wouldn't kill his mother, but she couldn't travel and that he could be his boy after
this. They killed and scalped her near the place known as
Betsy's run, which was named from her, and made off with
Charles into Ohio, where he lived with them until he was twenty-seven years old. While with them he was one of them, and
when very young married an Indian squaw, and from her had
four children, two boys and two girls. At the Morgan treaty
at the mouth of the Little Muskingum, James Hays was one of
the men under Levi Morgan, and inquired of the Indians as to
the whereabouts of his brother, Charles Drygoo, on which he
was informed that he was dead, but that he had some children.
He asked for them and he was given the two boys. He
brought them to where the town of Lot stands, where they
lived and died in the cabin built by James Hays in 1805. There
are a number of people in Wetzel county who are proud to say
that the blood of Charles Drygoo and his Indian squaw floats
in their veins.

MASSACRE OF THE HANDSUCKER FAMILY.

In the latter part of June, 1790, a party of Indians invaded a settlement on Dunkards creek, in Monongalia county, early in the morning. Mr. Clegg and Mr. Handsucker and his two sons were engaged at work near a house, when a band of Indians, concealed in bushes, shot at them and wounded Handsucker severely, and he was soon overtaken. Clegg and Handsucker's two sons began to run toward the house and Clegg entered it and defended it for a while. But confident that he would soon be driven out by fire he surrendered on condition that they would spare his life and that of his little daughter with him. The boys passed the house, but were overtaken by some of the savages, who were concealed in the direction they ran, and who had just taken Mrs. Handsucker and her infant captive. They then burnt the house, caught all the horses they needed, and made off with the prisoners, leaving one of their company as usual to watch after their retreat. When Mrs. Clegg heard the firing of a gun in the corn field, she was some distance from the house, and on hearing the shot immediately went to. ward the creek and concealed herself among the bushes and stayed until everything became quiet. She then crept out, and perceiving the Indian, began to run; he having seen her at the same time, took after her, but had to give up in despair. He shot at her, knowing that he would never catch her, but did not hit her, and she kept on running until she got safely off. Mr. Handsucker and his wife and child were killed on what is now known as Handsucker Knob, Wetzel county, at the forks of Dunkard and Fish creeks. Mr. Clegg, after remaining a captive among the Indians for some time, was released, on which he ransomed his two daughters.

HARMAN BLENNERHASSETT

Harman Blennerhassett, whose connection with the ill-fated project of Aaron Burr, has given his name a wide notoriety, passed down the Ohio river, in Wetzel county, on his way to Marietta, in 1796. About the year of 1798 he commenced his improvements on the beautiful island since known by his name, embosomed on the Ohio near the end of Washington county, Ohio, and resided upon it for a number of years, surrounded with all that made life dear, when the tempter entered this Eden and forever blighted his earthly prospects. After years of wandering he finally died in 1822, on the island of Guernsey. His beautiful and accomplished wife subsequently returned to this country and preferred charges against the United States and asked for claims, but without success. She died in New York in 1842. She was possessed of a rare ingenuity in the literary line and wrote that beautiful poem, "The Deserted Isle." The island will ever remain a memento of the fate of this unfortunate family, around whose melancholy fortunes the genius of Wirt his weaved a tribute of eloquence alike imperishable.

VOLNEY'S TRAVELS IN WETZEL.

In the latter part of the eighteenth century the celebrated French traveler Volney, traveled through Virginia and crossed the river into Monroe county, Ohio, near New Martinsville. He was under the guidance of two Virginia bear hunters through the wilderness. The weather was very cold and severe in crossing the dry ridge on the Virginia side. The learned infidel became weak from cold and fatigue. He was in the midst of an almost boundless wilderness, deep snow under his feet, and both rain and snow were falling upon his head. He frequently insisted on giving up the enterprise and dying where he was, but his comrades, more accustomed to the backwoods fare, urged him on until he at length gave out, exclaiming: "Oh, wretched and foolish man that I am, to leave my comfortable home and fireside, and come to this unfrequented place, where the lion and tiger refuse to dwell and the rain hurries off. Go on, my friends; better that one man should perish than three." Then they stopped and struck a fire, built a camp of bark and limbs, shot a buck, broiled the ham, which, with the salt bread and other necessaries they had, made a good supper, and everything being soon comfortable and cheery, the learned Frenchman was dilating largely and eloquently upon the ingenuity of man.

NOTES ON THE DEATH OF LOGAN'S FAMILY.

The following is taken from Jefferson's "Notes on Virginia:"

In April, 1774, a number of people being engaged in looking out for settlements on the Ohio, information was spread among them that the Indians had robbed some of the land jobbers, as those adventurers were then called. Alarmed for their safety, they collected together at Wheeling creek. Hearing that there were two Indians and some traders a little above Wheeling, Captain Michael Cresap, one of the party, proposed to way-lay and kill them. The proposition, though opposed, was adopted. A party went up the river with Cresap at their head, and killed the two Indians. The same afternoon it was reported that there was a party of Indians on the Ohio, a litle below Wheel-ing. Cresap and his party immediately proceeded down the river and encamped on the bank. The Indians passed them peaceably, and encamped at the mouth of Grave creek, a little below. Cresap and his party attacked them and killed several. The Indians returned the fire and wounded one of Cresap's men. Among the slain of the Indians were some of Logan's family. Zane expressed a doubt of it, but Smith, one of the murderers, said they were known and acknowledged that Lo-gan's friends and the party themselves generally said so, and boasted of it in the presence of Captain Cresap, and pretended no provocation, and expressed their expectations that Logan would probably avenge their death. Pursuing these examples, Daniel Greathouse and one Tomlinson, who lived on the oppo-site side of the river from the Indians, and were in the habit of friendship with them, collected at the house of Polke, on Cross run, about sixteen miles fromBaker's fort bottom, a party of thirty-two men. Their object was to reach a hunting camp of the Indians, consisting of men, women and children, at the mouth of Yellow creek, some distance above Wheeling. They proceeded, and when they arrived at Baker's station they concealed themselves among the bushes, and Greathouse crossed the river to the Indian camp. Baker tells us, being among them as a friend, he counted them and found them too strong for an open attack with his force. While here he was cautioned by one of the women not to stay, for the Indian men were drinking, and having heard of Cresap's murder of their relations at Grave creek, were angry and she pressed him in a friendly manner to go home, whereupon, after inviting them to come over and drink, he returned to Baker's inn, and desired that whenever any of them should come to his house he would give them as much rum as they would drink. When his plot was ripe, and a sufficient number were gathered at Baker's and intoxicated, he and his party fell upon them and massacred the whole, except one little girl, whom they preserved as a prisoner. Among these was the very woman who saved his life by urging him to retire from the drunken wrath of her friends, when he was spying their camp at Yellow creek. Either she or some other murdered woman was the sister of Logan. The party on the other side of the river, alarmed for their friends at Baker's, on hearing the report of the guns, made two canoes and sent them over. They were received as they appeared on the shore by a well-directed fire from Greathouse's party, which killed some and wounded others and obliged the rest to retreat. Baker tells us there were twelve killed and eight wounded. It was after this that Logan made his famous speech, which is as follows:

"I appeal to any white man to say if ever he entered Logan's cabin hungry, and I gave him not meat; it he came cold or naked, and I clothed him not. During the course of the last

long and bloody war Logan remained in his cabin, an advocate
of peace.   I had such affection for the white people that I was
pointed at by the rest of my nation.   I should have ever lived
with them had it not been for Col. Cresap, who last year cut
off in cold blood all the relations of Logan, not sparing my
women and children.   There runs not a drop of my blood in
the veins of any living creature.   This called upon me for vengeance.   I have sought it.   I have killed many and fully glut-
ted my revenge.   I am glad there is a prospect of peace on
account of the nation, but I beg you will not entertain a
thought that anything I have said proceeds from fear.   Logan
disdains the thought.   He will not turn on his heel to save
his life.   Who is there to mourn for Logan?   Not one." Logan gave all the blame to Colonel Cresap.   Whether he was
all to blame or not, it was one of the most inhuman massacres
that ever occurred in the border life.   Greathouse was afterwards killed by the Indians, but he deserved a greater punishment than that.

THE BATTLE OF CAPTINA.

Jefferson, in his "Notes on Virginia, says the battle of Captina was fought on the Virginia side in 1794, and it is probable that he is wrong, for Martin Baker told the author of the history of Ohio (McDonald) the following: He was twelve years of age when the battle of Captina was fought. Now Captina is a considerable stream entering the Ohio at Powhatan, on the Ohio side, and on its banks, says Martin Baker, the battle of Captina was fought. The following is the incident which fell from the lips of Martin Baker: One mile below the mouth of Captina, on the Virginia shore, was Baker's fort, so named from my father. One morning in May, 1794, four men were sent over, according to the custom, to the Ohio side to reconnoitre. They were Adam Miller, John Daniels, Isaac McCowan and John Shoptaw. Miller and Daniels took up stream and the other two down. The upper scouts were soon attacked by Indians, and Miller was killed. Daniels run up Captina about three miles, but being weak from loss of blood ensuing from a wound in his arm, was taken prisoner, carried into captivity, and subsequently released, at the treaty of Greenville. The lower scouts having discovered signs of the enemy, Shoptaw swam across the river and escaped, but McGowen, going up toward the canoe, was shot by Indians in ambush. Upon this he ran down toward the bank and sprang into the water, pursued by the enemy, who overtook and scalped him. The firing being heard at the fort they beat up the volunteers. There were about fifty men in the fort. There being much reluctance among them to volunteer, my sister exclaimed that she wouldn't be a coward. This aroused the pride of my brother, John Baker, who before had determined not to go. He joined the others, fourteen in number, including Captain Enochs. They soon crossed the river and went up Captina in single file a distance of about a mile and a half, following the Indian trail. The enemy had conceded that they were on their trail and were in ambush on the hillside awaiting their approach. When sufficiently near they fired upon them, but being on an elevated position their balls passed over them. The whites then treed some of the Indians, who then shot again and hit Captan Enochs and Mr. Hoffman. The whites then retreated and the Indians pursued but a short distance. On their retreat my brother was shot in the hip. Determined to sell his life as dearly as possible, he drew off to one side and secreted himself in a hollow with a rock at his back, offering no chance for the enemy to approach but in front. Shortly after two guns were heard in quick succession. Doubtless one of them was fired by my brother and from the signs afterwards it was supposed he had killed an Indian. The next day the men turned out and visited the spot. Enochs, Hoffman and my brother were found dead and scalped. Enoch's bowels were torn out, and his eyes and those of Hoffman screwed out with a wiping stick. The dead were wrapped in white hickory bark and buried in their bark coffins. There were about thirty Indians engaged in this, and seven skeletons were found of their slain, long after, secreted in the crevices of the rocks. McAuthor, after the death of Captain Enochs, was called on to lead the company. The Swaney chief, Charley Wilkey, lead the Indians.

David Prunty was the first man to open up a road in Wetzel county. He opened one from Middlebourne, Tyler county, to Reader, Wetzel county, in the year of 1815. The road is now known as eight mile ridge road.

In the year of 1790, a man by the name of Turbal erected a

grist mill near the present sight of the Wetzel county poor farm.

The first mail carried to Wetzel county was carried in the year of 1800, from Fairmont, now Marion county, to New Mar tinsville.

The first two-story log house along Big Fishing creek was erected by James Lowe, in the year of 1791.

In the year of 1790, George Wade erected a grist mill in what is now Clay district, and run it by water power; it was built of logs in the old style and for a long time did all the grinding that was to be done for miles around. A two log saw mill was erected by John Leaf in the year of 1835 in Proctor district. In the year of 1846 John Sole erected a grist and saw mill combined and run it by water power; the burrs were made of native stone, but did good work.

The pioneer of Grant district was John Wyatt, who came there in the year of 1790. He was followed by James Lowe, Uriah Morgan, James Jolliffe, and a man by the name of Wilson.

The first in Green district was James Troy, who settled on what is now known as the nergo quarters about the year of 1791. The property was transferred by him to Benjamin Rea- der, and from him to Morgan Morgan, who erected a house on the ground in the year of 1804, which stood until the year of 1897. Other settlers of Green district were James Hays, Wil- liam Snodgrass, Benjamin Hays, Z. Cochran, Aiden Bales, Jas- per Strait and many others.

The pioneer of Center district was Benjamin Bond, who set- tled there in the year of 1805.

The first settler in Clay district was William Little, who settled where the town of Littleton now stands in the year of 1810.

The first settler in Church district was Henry Church, who came there in the year of 1782 and settled where the town of Hundred now stands.

GEORGE BARTRUG.

George Bartrug, from whom Burton should have been named, was born in what was then known as Croach Back, Pennsylvania, in the year of 1790. He came with his parents to what is now known as Cottontown in the year of 1806. After living with them but a short time he married and erected a cabin near the present site of the B. & O. R. R. station at Burton, and lived there until the year of 1850, when the railroad company purchased the land. He erected another house on the land now owned by his son Moses Bartrug, and the house stood until lately, when it burned down.

PRESSLEY MARTIN.

Pressley Martin was born in Martin's Fort, in Monongalia county, in which his father at that time was commander. He came to what is now New Martinsville in the year of 1808, and boarded at the house on the south of the forks of the creek and the Ohio river, which was then owned by Abraham Hanes. In 1810 he purchased the land on which is now situated the town of New Martinsville from Mrs. Dulin, the widow of Edward Dulin, and erected a house on the north forks of Big Fishing creek and the Ohio river, which was commonly known as the Point House, on which is now situated the Grand Opera House, and the place of business of Handron & Dulin. He carried the nails that he put in the house from Morgantown to New Martinsville in pack saddles, they having been made at that place by a blacksmith. A short time after purchasing the land, he married Miss Margaret Clinton. While living at that place he farmed the land on which is now situated the prosperous town of New Martinsville, and often made trips to the Kanawha river for salt. In 1836 he laid out the town of New Martinsville and named it Martinsville, and in the incorporating of the town the Assembly of Virginia prefixed the word New before the Martinsville, making it New Martinsville, from the fact htat there was a town in Henry county, Va., by that name. He died in the year of   His name will always be remembered as the originator of the town of New Martinsville.

HENRY CHURCH.

Henry Church, better known as "Old Hundred," was born in Suffox county, England, in 1750. He came to this country a British soldier of the 63rd Light Infantry, and served under Lord Cornwallis in the memorable campaign of 1791. He was captured by the troops under Lafayette and sent a prisoner to Lancaster, Pennsylvania. He remained there until peace was declared at that place. He fell in love with a Quaker maiden, Miss Hannah Kiene. She was born in the year of 1755. Henry Church lived to be one hundred and nine, and his wife one hundred and seven. When the first excursion train ran over the B. & O. R. R. in 1852, it made a stop at the home of "Old Hundred," and among the passengers was an attache to the British legation at Washington City, who was introduced to the old man as one of his countrymen, who sounded one of the martial airs of England. "Old Hundred" stood up as though his blood had been warmed with wine, and said: "I know it, I know it!" He was loyal to his king for more than a hundred years, about which time he took allegiance to the United States. The home of "Old Hundred" stood near Main street, at Hundred, and was constructed from logs. They had eight children, the youngest dying at sixty-eight, on which "Old Hundred" made the remark that they never did expect to raise her; that she never was a healthy child. It seemed that every family of the Churches honored one by naming it Henry, until there was Henry Church, Henry Church, Sr., who was not "Old Hundred," Henry, Jr., who was not the youngest, Henry of Henry, Henry of Sam, Long Henry and Short Henry. They both are buried at Hundred.

ABRAHAM HANES.

Abraham Hanes was born in Louden county, Virginia, in the year of 1784. He came from that place to Middle Island creek, Tyler county, in the year of 1804, where he married Susana Martin a native of New Jersey. In 1807 they came to what was then the mouth of Big Fishing creek, and erected a house on the South Side, and kept hotel during the war of 1812 in the same house that was known to the citizens of the county as the Robert Cox homestead. The ground is now owned by Dr. Underwood. In 1814 he moved with his family one mile below Proctor, and built a house on a run which now bears his name.

SAMPSON THISTLE.

Sampson Thistle was born in Alleghenv county, Maryland, in the year of 1781, June 27th. He came to Tyler county, Virginia, now Wetzel county, West Virginia, in the year of 1805. In the year of 1806 he was married to Susana Tomlinson, at the home of the bride in Cumberland, Maryland, in a brick house, which is still standing, and in excellent condition. After the close of the usual festivities incident to such occasions in those days, they started on horseback to their future home near New Martinsville, where they maintained a comfortable and hospitable home the remainder of their days. He was a prominent and prosperous citizen, being deferred to by his neighbors and becoming the owner of much land. This worthy couple raised a family of eleven children, six sons and five daughters, all of whom attained maturity, were married and left the parental roof before their parents died. Sampson Thistle lived to the age of seventy-five years, and was buried in the family burying-ground on his farm, whither the body of his faithful wife was borne a few years later at nearly the same age. Of their large family only one is now living. He was a "Whig" in politics, in religion a Methodist. The land upon which he lived is situated ten miles north of the town of New Martinsville, comprising nearly 900 acres, and is now owned by his grandchildren.

R. W. COX.

Robert Woods Cox was born in the year of 1820 at the Old Robert Woods homestead six miles above Wheeling. He was six years old when his mother died, and shortly afterward the family removed to New Martinsville Tyler county, now Wetzel county. He attended law college at Meadville, Pennsylvania. but never was admitted to the bar, for the reason that he had to assume the care of his real estate. He assisted his father in the mercantile business. He was interested in the welfare and development of Wetzel county and was a great factor in politics. He was married in 1845 to Miss Jane Cresap, who was from one of the oldest settlers in the Ohio Valley, her father settling in Tyler county in the year of 1805. He sold his interest in Wetzel county in 1869, and went to Marshall county, where he died ten years later. His widow still survives him, at the age of seventy-nine. He had three children who are all dead with the exception of Friend Cox, who is still living.

JOHN MOORE.

John Moore was born August 24, 1818, at Clarington, Monroe county, then known as Sunfish, in the year of 1818. In the year of 1834 he came with his father, Jacob Moore, to Proctor, where he settled at the mouth of Proctor creek. At that time Proctor was a vast wilderness. He was justice in his district for twenty-five years and was also president of the county court for two terms. He is still living and is good for a number of years, and is recognized as one of the oldest living settlers in Wetzel county.

HON. JOHN M. LACEY,
Congressman from Iowa.

HON. JOHN F. LACEY.

John F. Lacey, representative in Congress from the Sixth Iowa district, was born May 30, 1841, on the Williams farm, just above New Martinsville, Va. (now West Virginia). In 1855 he moved to Iowa, and has made his home in Mahaska county ever since. At the beginning of the Civil War, in May, 1861, he enlisted as a private in Company "H," Third Iowa Infantry· afterward made a corporal. He was taken prisoner at the battle of Blue Mills, Mo., in September, 1861, and was paroled with General Mulligan's command at Lexington, Mo., soon after. The President issued an order for the discharge of all paroled prisoners, not then deeming it proper to recognize the Confederates by exchange. Mr. Lacey was discharged under this order. In 1862 an exchange of prisoners was agreed on, which released all discharged men from their parole, and Mr. Lacey at once re-enlisted as a private in Company "D," Thirty-third Iowa Infantry. He was soon promoted to the rank of sergeant-major of the regiment, and in May, 1863, was appointed first lieutenant of Company "C." Colonel Samuel A. Rice, of the Thirty-third Iowa, was made a brigadier-general, and Mr. Lacey was appointed by President Lincoln as assistant adjutant-general of volunteers on his staff. General Rice was killed at the battle of Jenkins Ferry, Ark., and Mr. Lacey was then assigned to the same position on the staff of Maj. Gen. Frederick Steele, in which capacity he served until his muster-out in September, 1865. He participated in the following battles: Blue Mills, Helena, Little Rock, Terre Noir, Elkin's Ford, Prairie d'Anne, Poison Springs, Jenkins Ferry, Siege of Mobile and storming of Blakeley. He was struck with a minie ball in the battle of Jenkins Ferry, but his ponche turned the ball aside and prevented any injury. His horse was killed under him by a shell in the battle of Prairie d'Anne.

Major Lacey's advancement was continuous, and although he was only twenty-four years of age at his discharge, he had in nearly four years' service done duty as a private, corporal, sergeant-major, first lieutenant, adjutant-general of a brigade, adjutant general of a division, adjutant general of a corps, adjutant general of General Steele's command (15,000 strong) in the Mobile campaign, and finally as adjutant general of Steele's Army of Observation (of 42,000 men) on the Rio Grande.

Mr. Lacey's education was obtained in the public schools and private academies. He was admitted to the bar in 1865, and has continually practiced law ever since, having enjoyed a very extensive practice in the State and Federal courts. He is the author of "Lacey's Railway Digest," which includes all the railway cases in the English language up to 1885; also author of "Lacey's Iowa Digest." He served in the Iowa Legislature in 1870, and afterward as alderman and city solicitor of Oskaloosa for a term each.

Notwithstanding his long service in Congress, he has retained his love for his profession, and kept up his connection with his law practice. He represented the sixth Iowa district in the Fifty-first, Fifty-third, Fifty-fourth, Fifty-fifth and Fifty-sixth Congresses. He is now a member of the Fifty-ninth Congress. This district has long been a political battle ground, and Mr. Lacey has had a hard contest in each of the campaigns in which he has been engaged. His opponents were General Weaver, Mr. White, Mr. Taylor and Mr. Steck, in these various campaigns. Though active in political affairs, Mr. Lacey has always preferred to be known through his chosen profession, rather than as a politician.

An old and eminent member of the State bar and one of Mr. Lacey's most intimate professional associates, submits this estimate of his character:

"As a lawyer, Mr. Lacey easily ranks among the leading lawyers of the State. His greatest success in life has been at the bar, and he still holds a good practice, although for ten years a member of Congress. His success has been attained largely by his indomitable energy and industry. He is particularly strong as a trial lawyer, being full of resources. When driven from one position he will seize another so quickly and support it by such ready reference to authorities, that he frequently bewilders his opponents and wins out on a new line, which seems to come to him by intuition as the trial progresses. As an advocate to the jury, he is not severely logical, not confining himself strictly to a mere reference to the evidence, but takes a wider range, and by illustrations drawn from literature or history, he retains the interest of the jury, while at the same time emphasizing some feature of the case."

Major Lacey is one of the Wetzel county boys who went west to grow up with the country. His father, John M. Lacey, was one of the first settlers of New Martinsville. He came to the town when it became the county seat and built the house now owned by Mr. McCaskey, immediately east of the court house. Major Lacey and Philip G. Bier both filled positions as assistant adjutant generals of volunteers. They were in the same class at school at New Martinsville when little boys.. Dr. John Thomas Booth, now of Concinnati, Ohio, was one of this same class. Dr. Booth was a surgeon in the Spanish war, and a Union soldier in the Civil War.

Mr. Lacey's mother was Eleanor Patten, daughter of Isaac Patten, of Captine creek, Belmont county, Ohio. She is held in pleasant memory by the old settlers. Major Lacey's parents both died in Iowa.

Robert W. Lacey, an uncle of John F., formerly lived in New Martinsville. He died in Pasadena, California, a few years ago. His widow is the sister of Mrs. Dr. Young, of New Martinsville.

Rev. J. J. Dolliver, father of Senator J. P. Dolliver, of Iowa, used to spend much of his time when a bachelor, at the home of

John M. Lacey, who was an active leader in the Methodist church.

Williams R. Lacey, the youngest son of John M. Lacey, was born in New Martinsville, and was named after the Williams family, who lived north of the town, and who were ardent friends of the Laceys. Williams R. is now the law partner of his brother, and is one of the most prosperous and successful business men in Iowa.

Mr. Lacey, in 1865, married Miss Martha Newell, of Oska-loosa. They have two daughters living, Eleanor, who is the wife of James B. Brewster, of San Francisco, and Berenice, who is now a young lady. Raymond, their only son, and Kate, another daughter, died in childhood.

We here give an address delivered by John F. Lacey, at Des Moines, Iowa, May 31, 1897:

FROM BULL RUN TO APPOMATTOX.

Comrades and Fellow Citizens:

I have come a long distance in compliance with the courteous invitation of my comrades of Kinsman and Crocker Posts to ad-dress you on this memorial day. To-day is a flower festival for the dead designed by General Logan, when he was the Com-mander in Chief of the Grand Army of the Republic.

Kinsman's and Crocker's names suggest memories of the past which bring pride and pleasure to every citizen of Des Moines, and of our whole State as well. Kinsman fell in battle, leading the 23d Iowa, but Crocker, though he died young, still lived to see victory crown our national cause.

We meet on this day with no political purpose, but lay aside all partisanship and forget for the time all matters of difference upon which we may be divided.

We assemble each year on this sad but pleasing memorial to· pass the old story down the line to another generation, and to keep alive the spirit of fraternity, charity and loyalty.

The new corn comes out of the old fields, and new lessons may always be learned by turning our eyes again upon the past.   Let us again revive

'The memory of what has been
But never more will be."

Every institution is the lengthened shadow of some great man who has passed away.   Our people have been led to great-ness by the hand of liberty.

The war was the penalty of a great wrong.   Individuals sometimes escape punishment in this world, because death claims them before the day of retribution comes.   But not so with nations—they cannot escape.   The wrong of slavery re-quired atonement, and severe, indeed, was the punishment that was meted out.

The men who fought against us recognized their first alle-giance as due to their States, and the soldier of the Union with a broader view felt that his country was the whole Union.   The war destroyed slavery and again restored the old sentiment of Patrick Henry when he said: "I am no longer a mere Virginian, I am an American."

We could not partition this Union.   We could not divide the Mississippi.   Bunker Hill and Yorktown were the heritage of the whole people.

We could not divide Yankee Doodle, nor could we distribute among the dismembered States the flag of our forefathers.

When the war began in 1861 we were twenty-six millions of freemen and four millions of slaves.   In 1897 we are seventy-millions, and all freemen.

When the body of Jefferson Davis was disinterred and re-moved to Richmond, the funeral train was witnessed by thou-sands as it passed through many States upon its long and final journey, but no slave looked upon that procession.

As I glance over this splendid audience here to-day I cannot help but feel that a country filled with such people is worth fighting for, and, if need be, worth dying for.

Kinsman died thirty-four years ago, but his name lingers upon all our tongues. Crocker passed to the great beyond later, but his name is still upon all our lips. The preservation of such a country is worth all that it cost in treasure, blood and tears.

There must be an appearance of right in everything to keep wrong in countenance, and our brothers of the South fought for their opinions with a zeal and earnestness that no men could have shown had they not felt that their cause was just. It is to-day the most pleasing of all things to hear one of these men say, "I now see that the result was for the best. I am glad that slavery has disappeared." Even Jefferson Davis in his history attempts to prove that the cause of the war was not slavery but the tariff. The day of peace and reconciliation has come, and no heart to-day in all this throng beats with anything but love for all who live under our flag. It is not mere emotional and meaningless sentimentalism, but brotherly kindness between the sections that were. There are no sections now.

Two ships may sail in opposite directions, moved by the same wind. But the course of all our people has now been directed to the same common goal. We meet in an era of reconciliation. The Grand Army has no vindictiveness. I will recall the war to-day, but will not seek to revive any of its bitterness. We should not forget it, but we should seek to keep alive none of its animosities.

If I bring back any of its horrors it is to the end that we may better appreciate peace. We renew the past to shun its errors.

The body of our great commander, Grant, has recently been enshrined in a new tomb erected by the free will offering of the people in the greatest city of our land, upon the beautiful Riverside Drive on the banks of the Hudson.

Napoleon lies in state under the gilded dome of the Invalides and his mausoleum is full of the inscriptions of his victories from Lodi to Marengo, from Austerlitz to Pena and Wagram, and even the abominable carnage of Essling is there commemorated.

But the silent commander of the Union army has a more noble inscription than if the names of all his battles had been there recorded. Over the door are his simple and touching words,

"Let us have peace."

Grant's victories made peace not only possible but permanent upon the only sure basis of union. The Potomac joins friendly States instead of separating hostile nations. It does not form a bloody boundary as the Tweed so long separated the land of our ancestors.

Grant should have been buried near Sheridan at Arlington with no sentinel but the stars, surrounded by the soldiers who had died under his command. Amid the stir and living bustle of the great metropolis his solitary grave seems lonely.

His example will live; obstinacy is the sister of constancy, and he never despaired of the Republic.

On a day like this we all recall such names as Lincoln, Grant, Sherman and Sheridan, but these names often all embrace our collective idea of the men whom they led. Their names typify their private soldiers. Thomas was the "Rock of Chickamaugua," because he knew how to command men who were brave enough to be led.

Buckner complained at Donelson of the demand for "unconditional surrender" as ungenerous terms. But he found that no terms were needed in surendering to so generous a foe. Grant was dangerous in fight, but he was kindness itself in victory.

When Lincoln's dead face was covered by Stanton, the great war secretary said, "He belongs to the ages." So with all the dead whom we commemorate to-day. Time mitigates sorrow and adds to the glory of events.

Michael Angelo buried his Cupid so that it might pass for an antique. Now a work of Michael Angelo is as precious as if made by Phidias himself.

The time of was is now sufficiently remote to be reviewed without prejudice. Who cares now for the assaults of Junius upon Lord Mansfield? Dennis made a burden of the life of Alexander Pope. All we know of him now is that he fretted Pope, and that his name was Dennis.

Who now heeds the abuse that was heaped upon the head of the mighty and patient Lincoln?

Rancor is dead with the dead, and malice does not go beyond the four edges of the grave.

We speak of these men because it is more interesting and pro-fitable to study the example of an illustrious man than an ab-stract principle.

When Lord Nelson was signaled to retreat at Copenhagen he turned the blind eye, that he lost at Calvi, towards the signal and said that he was unable to make it out, and justified his disobedience by a great victory.

The people, young and old, are gracious to the soldiers of every war. Early in the present century a veteran who fought at Stony Point was indicted for some violation of law. His at-torney succeeded in getting the fact in evidence that the de-fendant had distinguished himself in that battle and made good use of it in his address to the jury. The verdict announced that "We, the jury, find the defendant not guilty because he fought at Stony Point." The court refused to receive the verdict in such a form, and the jury again retired and brought in another verdict of simple acquittal. But as they were about to retire the foreman said to the court, "Your honor, I am directed to say that it was lucky for the defendant that he fought at Stony Point." The same spirit has always actuated a free people, When Aaschylus was being tried and his life hung in the bal-ance, his brother stepped forward and drew aside the prisoner's cloak and showed the stump of the arm that he had lost in the defence of his country. The mute appeal was stronger than any spoken words, and the prisoner went free.

At this time the period we commemorate seems as remote to the new generation as the battles of ancient Greece and Rome. We think of the men who fought in the Revolution and the war of the Rebellion as old. It is hard to realize how young these men were.

I occasionally go into the museum of the dead letter office at Washington and look over the album of war photographs which were taken from the unclaimed letters of that day. The young features of those soldiers look out from the past as a revelation. The sight of the kind and boyish faces from the school and farm, the shop or the store, and the new ready-made, misfit uniforms in which they were clad carried me back to the days when as a boy I went to the front with comrades such as these. Two brothers sitting side by side in their army clothing, sent their picture to their friends, but in vain.

A young sergeant standing by the side of his little sister is among these lost photographs, and the fresh young face and curls of the girl of thirty-five years ago would make us think that one of our own daughters had sat for the picture, were it not for the fact that she is clad in the fashions of another generation.

Another young private and a lady who is evidently his wife look out from the dead past in this album in the museum; and for hours you may gaze and find the youthful eyes of the boys of 1861 again looking at you. But we glance in the glass as we pass out and may well say:

'Time has stolen a march on me
And made me old unawares."

We may take an invoice of our gains and losses but our years never decrease.

When invited by Kinsman and Crocker Posts to address you on this occasion I was about to take a few days' journey through the battle fields of Virginia. These once horrid scenes are now as placid as the prairies of our own loved and beautiful Iowa, save where the earthworks remain as monuments of the past. Peace covers over the field with living green, and seeks to obliterate even the memories of blood.

In all ages a lion and a mound have thought to be a proper memorial for one of these historic battlefields.

The Greeks at Cheronea twenty-two hundred years ago marked that fatal scene with a mound over the graves of their dead and surmounted it with a lion, the broken remains of which are there at this day.

Where Napoleon's old guard died at Waterloo is a gigantic mound two hundred feet high and surmounted by the great Belgian lion, cast from captured cannon.

When I visited that spot a few years ago the straw of a dove's nest hung from the lips of the lion and peace had taken possession of the very symbol of war. At Cheronea a traveler says he found the honey of a wild bee in the mouth of the broken statue, as Sampson found the honey in the carcass of a dead lion in days of old.

We are strong enough to preach and practice the gospel of peace and arbitration. Speed the day when the prophesy of Isaiah may be fulfilled:

"The wolf also shall dwell with the lamb, and the leopard shall lie down with the kid; and the calf and the young lion and the fatling together; and a little child shall lead them.

"And the cow and the bear shall feed; their young ones shall lie down together; and the lion shall eat straw like the ox.

"And the sucking child shall play on the hole of the asp; and the weaned child shall put his hand on the cockatrice den.

"They shall not hurt nor destroy in all my holy mountain; for the earth shall be full of the knowledge of the Lord as the waters cover the sea."

So in the once hostile and bloody fields of Virginia all now is peace, but the scarred bosom of the earth still tells the story of 1861 to 1865.

Perhaps it would interest the young people as well as the old soldiers to hear some brief description of these well known scenes.

The soldier of the west by such a visit will better realize the heroism of his comrade in arms in the eastern armies. No one can look over the scene of the conflicts in Virginia without according to our comrades of that army the full mead of praise which brothers should always award to the achievements of each other.

As a crow flies it is only 120 miles from Bull Run to Appomattox. Measured in time it was a journey of nearly four years.

Measured in blood and tears it was a thousand years.

The journey was by various and devious routes; through mud and mire, through sunshine and through storm, through summer heats and winter snows, through dangers by flood and fire, through dangers by stream and wood, through sickness and sorrow; and by the wayside death always stalked grimly and claimed his own.

Twice did Bull Run witness the defeat of the cause of the National Union. It was indeed a fatal field to the federal army. When we approached that historic spot from Manassas Junction we met a large number of negro children on the road in holiday attire going to the "breaking up of school."

Had Appomattox not closed what Bull Run so disastrously began there would have been no school for these colored boys and girls. They were the living evidences of the changes that were brought about by the fearful journey which the Union troops traveled before the humiliation of Bull Run was atoned for by "peace with honor" at Appomattox. The two hundred years of enforced ignorance must now be compensated by the privileges of education.

President Lincoln came into the Nation's capital in the night to take the oath of his high office.

Sumter was the scene of the first encounter, but it was at Bull Run that the greatness of the contest upon which we had entered first was realized.

The confederates gave this battle the more euphonious name of Manassas. It was their victory, and they had a right to name it, but yet in history it will no doubt remain as Bull Run until the end of time.

In the open field at Henrv's farm we were reminded of the struggle that here terminated in defeat to the national cause. Here General Bee was killed, and before he fell he pointed to General Jackson's brigade and said: "There stands Jackson like a stone wall," and ever after the brigade was called by the name suggested, and its gallant commander was known as "Stonewall Jackson."

It is not far to Chancellorsville, where two years later this confederate fell upon the battle field, and as his life ebbed away, murmured, "Let us cross over the river and rest under the shade of the trees." The spot at Chancellorsville is marked with a granite monument, and the confederate soldier, Captain Talioferro, who pointed it out to me with tears in his eyes: "I loved that man. I was wounded four times while I was under his command. I mourned his death then, but I see it all now. It is all for the best. If he had lived the Union could not have been restored. It is better as it is." Whilst I do not believe that one man, however great, could have made the success of the rebellion sure, yet it is true, not excepting Lee himself, there was no man whose life was so vital to the rebel cause as that of Stonewall Jackson.

But to return to Bull Run battle field. Standing where Jackson was wounded, the Henry house is near by. An old lady, Mrs. Henry, was in that house when the first battle began. She was bed-ridden, and eighty-five years of age. No one thought there would be a battle there, but supposed it would

At Richmond the marks of war abound, and the approaches and defences are still shown by trenches and parapets.

In all these Virginia battle-grounds the pits showing the empty graves of soldiers whose remains had been transferred to some national cemetery are to be seen on every hand as a horrid reminder of the past.

Petersburg, with its ten months siege, invited our careful attention, and the remains of the ghastly crater where so many men, white and black, were slaughtered as they huddled together in the deep hole, from which they could neither advance nor retreat.

At Spottsylvania we met a party of Virginia school girls who had come twenty-five or thirty miles to see the famous region, and they were looking at the fine monument built by the Sixth Corps to commemorate the death of Segwick, their commander general. We told them that we were going on to Appomattox, and they said they were glad the war was over, but that they could not bear to think of looking at Appomattox.

Staying over night at a hospitable home near the Wilderness, we were entertained with accounts of dark days of the war. One lady told us with some of the old tone of remonstrance how the Yankees drove away her cattle against her indignant protest.

An old confederate who joined in the conversation said their soldiers were much more considerate and honest, for when they went to Gettysburg they paid or offered to pay for everything — in confederate money.

But let us hasten on to the end where peace spreads her wings again, where Grant gave back to Lee's army their cavalry and artillery horses to use in plowing the neglected fields of the South. He treated them as our countrymen and then and there laid deep the foundation of respect and confidence that, let us fondly hope, will grow stronger and more cemented with the coming years.

Now and then some discordant bray is heard in the general peace, and some one not particularly noted in the war seems ready to fight it all over again now after it has passed into history. But fortunately this sentiment is small and growing less and less.

In the last congress a fire eating congressman wanted to try it on again, and announced that he was ready to renew the contest on a moment's notice, when one of my confederate friends came over to me and, rolling up his sleeve, said: "Do you see that saber cut?" Turning his face he then showed me a bullet scar near his ear and said: "I have two more of these mementoes on my left leg, and I have got through with my part of it, and the gentleman now speaking may fight it out alone next time, as he did not do much of it when he had the chance."

The Appomattox field is marked with tablets, so that in a visit there you may know when you are standing upon the exact spot where one of the great events of that memorable scene occurred.

Speculative vandalism has done its work and the Surrender House has been torn down and the brick and lumber marked and piled up ready for removal to some other place, there to be again set up as a show house to be exhibited for gain.

But the memories of Appomattox cannot thus be removed. The house at some distant city would be out of place. Appomattox Mountain could not be seen from its doors. Here a marker shows where Grant and Lee met; there another where the famous apple tree once stood; another where Grant set up his headquarters for the last time in the presence of an armed foe; here Lee read his last orders to his troops as they massed around him; and most interesting of all, here is marked the place where the hostile arms were stacked to be used no more against brethren forever.

Best of all there is no great charnel house at Appomattox. Nineteen graves show that the confederate armies gathered their dead together there, and in doing so they found one skeleton in blue that by oversight had not been removed to a distant national cemetery, and this Union soldier now lies buried side by side in the little cemetery of the confederate dead, and his grave is annually decorated with those of the men with whom he died on this historic field.

As we turn from the scene where the curtain rang down thirty-two years ago upon the final act of the greatest drama the world has ever seen, the full moon rose and soon

'The woods were asleep and the stars were awake,"
and only the note of the whip-poor-will dusturbed the solemn silence.

In looking around to-day over this assembly we mourn more and more the friends of our youth. Where are our comrades of 1861? Where are those who broke ranks with us in 1865? We meet some of them here today, grizzled and gray, and with young hearts yet, but alas, how many have fallen out by the way!

We miss and mourn them

"And the stately ships go on
    To their haven under the hill,
But, O for the touch of a vanished hand,
    And the sound of a voice that is still.
Break, break, break,
    At the foot of thy crags, oh Sea—
But the tender grace of a day that is dead
    Will never come back to me."

JONATHAN P. DOLLIVER.

J. P. Dolliver was born near Kingwood, Preston county, Va., now West Virginia, February 6, 1858. In 1875 he graduated from the West Virginia University at Morgantown. In 1854 he came to New Martinsville, Wetzel county, West Virginia, with his father, who was the first preacher that ever preached in a church at New Martinsville, and to his work and energy the building of the old M. E. church is due. His name will ever live to the members of that church. Mr. Dolliver was admitted to the bar in 1878, but never held any political office until elected as a Republican to the Fifty-first Congress as a representative from the Tenth Congressional district, and was elected again to the Fifty-second, Fifty-third, Fifty-fourth, Fifty-fifth and Fifty-sixth Congress. On July 22, 1900, he was appointed Senator to fill the unexpired term of Hon. J. H. Gear, deceased, and took his seat in the United States Senate December 3, 1900, which office he still holds. He is living in Iowa near the same locality as Hon. J. F. Lacey, another Wetzel county boy.

SENATOR J. P. DOLLIVER,
Senator from Iowa.

his own interests to serve a friend, and disliked to distress those who became indebted to him; so that, where others would have become wealthy, he remained comparatively poor. His family, however, have a far richer legacy in the unsullied character he sustained, and in the blessing of those "who had reaped his fields and whose wages he kept not back."

Coming here when this county was a wilderness, he lived to see a radical change in the character and appearance of the Ohio Valley, and in the manners and character of the population.

The judgment of the world in regard to a man's character, while he is living, is apt to be too harsh—his faults are magnified and his virtues overlooked; but when he is dead, the reverse is the case, and it is his faults which are forgotten and his virtues that are magnified. "The good we do lives after," and "the grave covers every fault and extinguishes every resentment." The verdict in the latter case may be much too mild and in the former it is too harsh; but of the subject of this sketch it can truthfully be said that he was a good citizen, an accommodating neighbor, an honest officer, a warm, faithful friend, a kind and affectionate husband and father; and if this does not include all his virtues, they are comprised in that other term to which he was so justly entitled, that of a "true Christian gentleman," and the world is better and happier because of his life.

EBENEZER CLARK.

Ebenezer Clark was born on Wheeling Creek, in Washington county, Pennsylvania, May 4th, 1802, and died at his home in the county of Wetzel, August 30th, 1878.

Perhaps no man was so long and so prominently identified with the history of the county with which we deal in this volume as the subject of the present sketch. When but an infant his father removed to the Scioto Valley, Ohio, afterwards going further West; but the boy, Ebenezer, then thirteen years of age, came to West Virginia, living with his mother's people in Marshall county. In early manhood he married and settled near Fanlight, in Wetzel (then Tyler) county, on what is now known as Clark's Ridge. Here the remainder of his life was passed.

Mr. Clark was one of the largest land owners in the county, and managed extensive business affairs with rare good judgment; but he was a public spirited man who was never so busy that he could not find time to devote to public affairs. For a generation, perhaps, he officiated as Justice of the Peace, under the old regime, when men served faithfully for honor and not for profit. Nature had given him a legal mind, and he easily grasped complicated cases, going unerringly to the heart of the controversy. In addition to this, few men in similar positions have attained as honorable distinction as a peacemaker. Countless controversies were brought to an end without litigation through his discreet advice and counsel, the universal confidence of the community in his integrity and sound judgment enabling him to make this most enviable record.

Before Wetzel county had come into being, Mr. Clark served as a member of the County Court of Tyler county; and for four years he was Sheriff of Wetzel, also serving his constituency faithfully at Richmond as a member of the Legislature of Virginia. Through his influence in that body a bill was passed providing for a turnpike road from New Martinsville to Burton. If carried through, this would have largely influenced the development of the county; but the project was defeated. through the jealousy of local politicians.

Mr. Clark's first wife was Harriet Anderson, and among their children are Josephus Clark, C. E. Clark, and Friend E. Clark, prominent citizens of Wetzel at the present time. His second wife was Mary Richmond, who, with their children, now resides in the State of Missouri.

The following was written of Mr. Clark at the time of his death by Robert McEldowney: "For almost fifty years he has been a prominent and influential citizen, and has left during all this period of public life not a blot on his fair name. In politics Mr. Clark was a Democrat of the old school, and in religion an old fashioned Methodist, who believed in experimental religion and was not afraid to say so. He was a prominent member of the Church for a half century and was for a generation a local preacher. He was a man hospitable and generous, fond of the truth and fearless in its defense and in the support of what he believed to be right. He was such a man as, take him all in all, we may not look upon his like again.

He was a strong man and a sincere Christian, whose memory is a benediction. His life brings to mind the lesson enforced by the greatest preacher of the nineteenth century: "Value the ends of life more than its means; watch ever for the soul of good in things evil, and the soul of truth in things false, and beside the richer influence that will flow out from your life on all to whom you minister, you will do something to help the solution of that unsolved problem of the human mind and heart, the reconciliation of hearty tolerance with strong positive belief."

ISAAC SMITH.

One of the most remarkable men in the history of West Virginia is Isaac Smith. At his death he was the oldest man in West Virginia, and probably the Southern States. He was born at Williamsport, Washington county, Pennsylvania, in the year of 1789, and lived to be 109 years old, which was but a few years back. He was a man of simple nature, kind, strong and always industrious. He lived until his death in Proctor Hollow, a ravine of five miles in length, running east and west through Wetzel county, in a small log cabin, about two miles from Proctor Station, on the Ohio River R. R. He erected the building with his own hands when he came to West Virginia with his family, sixty-nine years before his death. Then the country was a wide forest, with only a few families scattered here and there over the country. His nearest neighbor was a man by the name of Hogan, who resided with his family five miles further up the run.

Some of the older residents who remember him when he was forty to fifty years of age, say he could lift a barrel of whisky and drink out of the bunghole, and that he has often picked up two barrels of salt set one upon the other at a single lift. But of these things Mr. Smith never boasted. He had a smile for everyone and enjoyed a good joke as well as any person. He followed the occupation of keel boating on the Monongahela river until he was forty years of age, when he sold out his property and moved to West Virginia. When he settled at Proctor there were few if any Indians remaining, and the only thing to be feared was from wild animals, catamounts, wild cats and a few wolves. There was also plenty of wild game. Mr. Smith's father settled at Elizabeth, Pa., in the latter part of

ISAAC SMITH.
109 Years Old.

the last century. His name was Samuel Smith, and he married Sallie Watt the result of which union was several sons,
among them being the subject of this sketch. Isaac Smith received very little education, but learned the trade of keel boating at an early age, which he followed many years. He married Sarah Hutson, and to them were born five sons, Robert,
Charles, Thomas, Samuel and John. Mr. Smith made his home
with his grandson, Albert Anderson, who lives on the old
homestead, where his mother was born and raised.

WILLIAM LITTLE.

William Little settled where Littleton now stands, on Fish creek, in the year of 1838, when it was a vast wilderness without a solitary being for miles around except that of his wife. He was born in Fayette county, this State, and for some time lived in Green county, Pennsylvania. He was justice of the Peace when this county was Tyler county for sixteen years. There are only three of the family now living H. H. Little who has been in the ministry for the past thirty-five years; Ruth Lancaster and James K. Little. William Little's brother, Josiah, was captain of artillery in the Mexican war.

JEREMIAH WILLIAMS.

Jeremiah Williams was one of earliest settlers in this county. He came to New Martinsville about the year of 1800, and settled on the land now owned by his heirs and situated about two miles above the town of New Martinsville. He was born in the year of 1766 and for a while was a Fort Henry soldier. He obtained the title for the land from a man in Monongalia county (for boot) on a horse trade, he having obtained it from a man who was driven out by the Indians. Mr. Williams witnessed the signing of the Declaration of Independence.

ROBERT McELDOWNEY, SR.

Robert McEldowney was born in Ireland and emigrated with his brother (John) to this country about the year of 1782, and settled on the land about one and a half miles north of the town of New Martinsville, and now owned by Mr. B. F. Bridgeman, in the year of 1804, having lived for a while at Buckhill Bottom, Ohio. His brother settled in Maryland, where his descendants still live. Mr. McEldowney died in a carriage. He was very feeble at the presidential election of 1844, and desiring to vote for Jamese K. Polk, a carriage was sent after him, and after getting in the carriage he suddenly died and was buried in Williams' Cemetery, where his wife, Hannah Vandaver McEldowney was buried.

H. R. THOMPSON,
Clerk of the County Court.

JUDGE THOMAS I. STEALEY.

In the History of Wetzel county, Judge Stealey should not be forgotten for the part which he took in the proceedings preliminary to the formation of the county by the act of the legislature of Virginia. The continued agitation of the re-location of the county seat of Tyler county from Middlebourne to Sistersville. caused the citizens of Middlebourne to take such a course as would put at rest the vexatious question and to that end the father of Judge Stealey, James Stealey, long since deceased, in connection with other citizens of Tyler county, held a meeting in the law office of J. M. Stevenson (then residing at Middle bourne), but subsequently an honored citizen of the city of Parkersburg, who at the election for president in 1844 was an elector on the Whig ticket, bearing the name at its head of the distinguished American Statesman, Henry Clay, the author of the protection tariff of 1845 and the compromise bill of 1853. This is not wholly a digression, for strange as it may seem, it was a wise act of strategy politically to hold a meeting in the office of a leading Whig such as was James M. Stevenson. It was intended at that time to nominate a Democrat as a candidate for the election to the Virginia Legislature. P. W. Martin, according to the Democratic party usage, was entitled at that time to the nomination for the office, but there had been local dissentions in the ranks of the party which made it unwise to select a man from that part of Tyler county in the person of P. M. Martin, a staunch Democrat of the Jeffersonian style, to be the candidate, and the friends of the measure, to divide Tyler county by making a new county (Wetzel), by a line striking off all of the northern

portion of Tyler county for that purpose, and thus get rid of
that part of the territory of the county that was in favor of the
re-location of the county seat, it became necessary to secure a
delegate who would advocate the new county in the legislature,
and James G. West, of the northern portion of the county, was
selected by James Stealey, James M. Stevenson, and Joseph
McCoy, two Whigs, and the last named a Democrat. A committee appointed to select a delegate by the Democratic meeting held in the law office of a leading Whig, after the nomination of James G. West by James M. Stevenson and James
Stealey, two Whigs, and Joseph McCoy, a Democrat. Judge
Stealey, then only fifteen years of age, was directed by said
nominating committee to prepare the notice required by law to
secure the formation of a new county, which was promptly
prepared and posted by him at many prominent places in the
county as required by law. After years the people of Wetzel
county remembered favorably the part taken by him in the
formation of the county by giving him a majority of 1,200 votes
over his opponent, the late distinguished Judge C. J. Stewart,
for the office of Judge in the Fourth Judicial Circuit, composed of the counties of Wetzel, Tyler, Doddridge and Ritchie
which position Judge Stealey held for a term of eight years,
discharging the duties thereof faithfully and with ability and
honor. Judge Stealey moved from New Martinsville in the
year 1889 to the city of Parkersburg, where he has since resided, engaging in the practice of law with great success, and
having accumulated a sufficient competency to live a quiet
life, he retired from the practice of his profession in 1898 and
is yet living at the age of 72, the picture of health and contentment, devoting much of his time to the study of the advanced
problems of science, history and economies.

OLD WETZEL COUNTY COURT HOUSE,
New Martinsville.

FORMATION OF WETZEL COUNTY.

Wetzel county was formed in 1846 from Tyler, by an act of the Assembly of Virginia; was named from Louis Wetzel a distinguished frontiersman and Indian scout (see Louis Wetzel). The first session of court was held in April, 1846, in the house then owned by Sampson Thistle, which was designated for the place by the legislature. It was situated on the corner of Main and Jefferson streets, and is now the property of Otto Soland. The officers of the court were Joseph L. Fry, judge; Friend Cox, clerk of the Circuit Court; Pressley Martin, clerk of the County Court; Edward Moore, crier of the court; James Snodgrass, attorney for commonwealth; Lewis Williams, surveyor. The justices were P. M. Martin, P. Martin, B. F. Martin, Wm. Anderson, P. Witten, F. E. Williams, Owen Witten, Andrew McEldowney, Samuel McEldowney, Hezekiah Alley, R. W. Cox. James Paden, Daniel Anderson, James Morgan, Henry Garner, J. V. Camp, Wm. Sharpneck and Stephen Carney. Wm. Sharpneck, being the oldest justice, was made sheriff. At each term of the County Court, three justices acted as commissioners of the County Court. The first to act were B. F. Martin, P. M. Martin, P. Martin, Wm. Anderson and P. Witten, with P. Martin as president. The deputy sheriffs were Charles McCoy and Archibald Thistle; the commissioners of revenue were Thomas Snodgrass, Sampson Thistle, Wm. Little, Ebenezer Payne, James G. West, Ebenezer Clark, Hezekiah Joliffe, James Ruckman, Isaac E. Haskinson, Wm. Anderson, John Alley, John Klepstein and Jacob Talkington. On April 7th, 1846, J. W. Stephens, C. W. Clark, W. J. Boreman, R. W. Lock, J. R. Morris, F. W. McConaughy, I. W. Horner, James Snodgrass, G. W. Thompson and Thomas Jones were permitted to practice law in the courts. On May 4th of the same year, Isaac Hoge, J. Morris and Abraham Samuels were permitted to practice law before the court. The house of Sampson Thistle was bought for $400, and R. W. Cox and B. F. Martin appointed to see that the court house was properly repaired, and to superintend the building of a jail. In 1848 the county had sufficient funds in the treasury to build a new court house, which they did, but it was not completed until the year of 1852. The ground where the court house and jail were built was donated by Sampson Thistle and Pressley Martin, and when the court house was completed it was pronounced one of the best houses of its kind in the State. Court was held in the building until 1900. The building was beginning to look shabby, it was behind the times, and was very inconvenient, and the county court, which consisted of James Joliffe, John De Bolt and Abe Fair gave the contract for the erection of a new building, which will cost about $100,000 when completed. The first grand jury appointed by Sheriff Sharpneck were John M. Lacey, foreman; Absalom Postlewait, Frances Hindman, Archiles Morgan, Hiram J. Morgan, James Cochran, Caleb Headlee, J. Van Camp, Jeremiah Williams, Thomas Stiel, Richard Postlethwait, Joseph Wood, Robert Leap, Zadoc L. Springer, Andrew Workman, John Roberts, Jacob Rice, Jacob McCloud, and Wm. Little. The first indictment brought against a person was the commonwealth against Elisha McCormick, for assault and battery. Wm. McDonald, a native of Cork, was the first man to be naturalized. The first trial before the County Court was the Commonwealth vs. Holden Cooper, upon his recognizance for a felony. The first estate settled in this county was the estate of C. B. Pitcher, of which J. C. Pitcher was administrator, and Friend Cox, Pressley Martin and B. F. Martin were appraisers. The estate amounted to $207.05.

On May 31, 1861, delegates from twenty-five counties in Virginia assembled at Wheeling and determined that they

W. F. SHUMAN,
Commissioner of the County Court.

would not take part in the war against the Union without the will of the people. The delegates from Wetzel county were Elijah Morgan, T. E. Williams, Josephus Murphy, Wm. Burrows, B. T. Bowers, J. R. Read, J. M. Bell, Jacob Young, Reuben Martin, R. Read, R. S. Sayre, W. D. Walker, Geo. W. Bier, Thos. McQuown, John Alley, S. Stephens, R. W. Lauck. John McCaskey, Richard Cook, Andrew McEldowney and B. Van Camp. The next convention was held June 11 of the same year. The members of this convention being elected, the others being appointed. The State was represented by thirty counties this time. At this convention Wetzel county sent James G. West, Reuben Martin and B. J. Ferrell. At this convention Francis H. Pierpoint was elected the first governor of the State. The third convention was held November 20 of the same year, for the purpose of reorganizing the government. The delegate from Wetzel county was R. W. Lauck, Another convention was held two years later, in 1863, at Charleston. It was under the new constitution. Septimius Hall was elected.

Officers of Wetzel county from the formation down to the present time:

Sheriffs—Wm. Sharpneck, Edwin Moore, Wm. Anderson, Josephus Clark, Levi Shuman, A. P. Brookover, W. M. Brookover, John Stender, B. B. Postlethwait, John Stender, J. N. Wyatt, James Pyles and Alex Hart.

Clerks of the County Court—Pressley Martin, J. W. Newman, Friend Cox, Z. S. Springer, J. D. Ewing, Z. S. Springer, H. E. Robinson, John C. McEldowney, the latter serving twenty-six years, having been appointed for two years, and Henry Thompson.

Clerks of the Circuit Court—Friend Cox, John C. McEldowney, J. W. Neewman and John Kauffman, Mr. Newman having served eighteen years.

Prosecuting Attorney—James Snodgrass, L. S. Hall, R. W. Leuck, Wm. Guthrie, George Boyd, L. S. Hall, M. R. Crouse. W. S. Wiley, M. R. Morris and E. L. Robinson.

COL. ROBERT McELDOWNEY

Robert McEldowney, of whom we present a fair likeness was one of the most widely known editors in the State. He was editor of the Wetzel Democrat and his writings were often quoted by some of the leading journals of the State. He was often referred to as the Bill Nye of West Virginia. He was born in 1837, at New Martinsville, and atended the schools at that place, later going to the Moundsville Academy and the Marietta College, but before graduating at Marietta he enlisted as a private in the Southern army and was later commissioned captain, commanding the Twenty-seventh Stonewall Brigade being twice wounded. He served until the close of the war. At the battle of Gettysburg he took charge of the wing of the army in which a general was killed, and led a part of the whole army at that place. He was the first teacher appointed by the board of education in Magnolia district. He was a member of the Legislature and was one of the delegates to the National convention that nominated Hancock for president. The last years of his life were passed in sufferings that were untold, and on —————————— he diedwith cancer of the tongue. Thus ended a life of usefulness, which was shortened by that dread affliction.

COL. ROBERT McELDOWNEY.

CAPT. JOHN McCASKEY.

Captain McCaskey was born in Steubenville Ohio February 19, 1834. When a boy he came with his parents to New Martinsville and continued to reside there until the war, when he enlisted in the army, and was electd first lieutenant in Company C, Fifteenth West Virginia. He was afterwards promoted to captain and commanded Company C in some of the hardest fought battles of the war. After he returned from the war in 1862, he was appointed Justice of the Peace, which office he held until his death. He was also receiver of both county and circuit courts. At one time he held the office of mayor of New Martinsville for a number of terms. While in the army he contracted pulmonary consumption, which caused his death, dying September 22, 1882.

ELIJAH MORGAN.

Elijah Morgan was born in Green district, Wetzel county, in the year of 1840. He was a delegate to the constitutional convention that determined that they would not take arms against the Union. He then enlisted in 1861 in Company H, First West Virginia Infantry, and remained in the army until the close of the war, taking part in some of the most important battles, and the last battle of Bull Run. He was not in the regiment long until he was commissioned sergeant. He was a grandson of Morgan Morgan, whose name has been frequently mentioned in this book.

ALEX. HART,
Sheriff of Wetzel County.

CAPT. BASIL T. BOWERS.

Basil T. Bowers was born in Cuyahoga county, O., in the year of 1837. In the year of 1861 he came to Wetzel county with the intention of studying law at that place. At this time the civil war was coming on and there was very little business for lawyers. Early in May of the same year he obtained authority to enlist volunteers for service in the United States army, and enlisted the first volunteers from Wetzel and Tyler counties, then Virginia. In Wetzel he enlisted George Dillon, Sam McCollough, Wm. Branford, C. Frankhouser, John Fouler, Henry Gehring, Felix Hill, David Kirkland, Leonard Roberts, James A. Robinson, and others. In Tyler he enlisted J. B. Smith Fred Garrison, Samuel Spencer, Wm. Gorrell, James Fardyce (who was probably the first Union soldier enlisted in Tyler county), Jackson Jounkins, R. D. Kelch, Marion Moore, Hiram White, James M. Kay, Peter D. Moore, Jacob Ritchie and others. These volunteers formed a part of Company E, Second regiment of Virginia volunteers, and were mustered into the United States service June, 1861 at Camp Carlisle, at Wheeling. Captain Bowers served in the United States army from 1861 until 1865, when he was mustered out at Brazos Santiago, Texas. After the war he returned to Wetzel county, where he has made his home ever since, engaged in his profession.

CAPT. FRIEND CLAY COX.

Wetzel county has produced no more knightly son or finer gentleman than Friend C. Cox, and this volume would be incomplete without a loving tribute to his memory

Friend C. Cox was the son of Friend Cox, a sketch of whose life we publish, and Susan Thistle Cox, his wife, and was born April 21st, 1844. The stirring events leading to the civil war between the States, which so profoundly stirred men's souls, made a man out of the boy of sixteen or seventeen, whose unusually handsome face and person and brilliant mind had already made him a leading figure in the life of both New Martinsville and the county. His influence had been felt in local politics, and the campaign of 1860 found him making ringing speeches for Breckenridge & Lane. Those were stirring days in Wetzel, and the outspoken sympathizer with the Southern cause soon heard rumors that his arrest had been planned by zealous Federal partisans, whose active efforts sent many embryo Confederates to Camp Chase and similar safe retreats.

But the activities of young Friend Cox were not to thus be confied. He promptly left home, telling his mother he intended to embark on the lower river, with a relative who owned a steamer; and, with Robert McEldowney and other brave spirits, he made his way to the Confederate lines. He enlisted as a member of the Shriver Grays, a company organized at Wheeling, and served through the war as a member of the immortal Stonewall Brigade.

Of Friend Cox, the soldier, we need not speak at length, for his record is one with that of the invincible battalion, whose achievements will be studied and analyzed as long as men learn the art and science of war and find inspiration in the record of

JOHN W. KAUFFMAN,
Clerk of Circuit Court.

heroic deeds. He knew not fear, and one who fought by his side has said that amid the whistle of bullets and the shriek of shells he was the genius of battle incarnate; and General James A. Walker, the last commander of the Brigade, in a recent letter to a personal friend, says of Captain Cox: "He was as brave as any knight who ever drew sword, and I loved him." Although the youngest of them all, he attained the highest rank of any of the sons of New Martinsville who served in the war. For gallant conduct on the field of battle he, by success-ive promotions, reached the position of Captain and Adjutant-General of the Stonewall Brigade, which rank he held at the time of the surrender. His war record is well epitomized in the sentence uttered at the time of his death by a leading news-paper man of West Virginia: "He bore the reputation of a gal-lant soldier and a valued officer."

Subsequent to the civil war Captain Cox engaged in business in Baltimore, St. Louis, and New York City. From the last named city he returned to his native town to die, having con-tracted consumption while in the army. His death occurred on the 26th day of January, 1876.

Handsome, courtly, knightly, loved and admired by his friends, both men and women, old Wetzel may well be proud that she produced him, and her younger sons may well emulate the vigor and intensity with which he met life's problems. This inadequate tribute can best be classed in the language of one of his dearest friends: "It is difficult for one who feels his loss as a personal bereavement, to write fittingly of the dead, much less to offer consolation to the living; but if gentleness and kindness, and courage and generosity, and all the virtues which make men esteem and love each other, are reckoned in the final settlement, our Friend will have a part in the first resurrec-tion."

JUDGE M. H. WILLIS.

Judge M. H. Willis, present Judge of the 4th Judicial Circuit, was born near Mole Hill, Ritchie county, W. Va., January 31, 1862. He received a sound English education, and at the age of sixteen began teaching school, during vacation being engaged in ordinary farm work. Later he attended the Harrisville High school, and subsequently the State University at Morgantown. His education was finished at the Northern Indiana Normal School at Valparaiso, Indiana, where he took a collegiate course, and was valedictorian of his class of seventy-six graduates. From this school Mr. Willis was graduated in 1886 with the degree of B. S. Having completed his studies he resumed teaching in Dakota, and later taught in Wisconsin. Having chosen law as a profession he in the meantime applied himself diligently to its study. In 1889 he came to West Union, and was for three years principal of the West Union graded schools. For two years he was principle of ... Wesley Academy at Berkeley Springs, W. Va., retaining, however, his residence in West Union.

Mr. Willis was admitted to the bar in 1890, and since the spring of 1893 has been actively engaged in the practice of law with success. His court papers are models of neatness and accuracy. As a counselor and adviser he is safe, reliable and conservative. He is a clear, thinker, a logical reasoner, and is regarded as one of the ablest advocates of the Doddridge county bar. Possessing thorough scholarship and an analytical mind, he closely investigates his cases and rarely forms a wrong conclusion. As showing the high regard in which he is held in his profession, it might be mentioned that at a recent term of the circuit court of Ritchie county in the absence of

JUDGE M. H. WILLIS,
Judge of the Fourth Judicial Circuit of West Virginia.

Judge Freer, he was chosen Special Judge of that court. His work as such commended itself to the bar and he was highly complimented by both press and bar for the fairness and accuracy of his decisions. In 1900 he was elected Judge of the Fourth Judicial Circuit, which position he still holds, performing the duties of said office with ability.

EX-JUDGE T. P. JACOBS.

No man of public life in Wetzel county is better known throughout the State of West Virginia than is Ex-Judge T. P. Jacobs, of New Martinsville. As a lawyer, judge and politician, he has won distinction and success. He was born near Cumberland Allegheny county, Maryland, in 1852, and his parents came to West Virginia when he was quite young. He secured his early education in the public and private schools of the State and graduated from the West Virginia University at Morgantown. Mr. Jacobs was elected Judge of the Fourth Judicial Circuit in 1888 as a Republican, which position he held until 1896. He is still living at New Martinsville, where he enjoys one of the finest residences in the county, devoting much of his time to the practice of his profession.

E. L. ROBINSON,
Prosecuting Attorney of Wetzel County.

BANKS OF WETZEL.

THE WETZEL COUNTY BANK.

It commenced business January 1st, 1890. W. S. Wiley is president; S. J. Elliott is vice president, and J. E. Bartlett is cashier. The bank has a capital of $35,000.00, and surplus of $28,929.30. W. E. Maple is assistant cashier. The directors are J. E. Bartlett, J. W. Leap, Henry Koontz, R. C. Standiford, S. J. Elliott, W. S. Wiley and C. C. Eisenbarth.

THE NEW MARTINSVILLE BANK.

It was opened June 1, 1897, with S. R. Martin as president, and J. W. Alderson as cashier. It has a stock of $25,000.00, surplus of $12,000.01. S. R. Martin is president; D. H. Cox is vice president; John A. Mandi is cashier; J. M. Schmied is assistant cashier. The directors are S. R. Martin, D. H. Cox, E. S. Duerr, F. W. Clark, J. W. Lentz, Wm. Ankrom and Charles J. Beck.

THE FIRST NATIONAL BANK

Began business the 21st day of March, 1900, with S. B. Hall as president; F. P. Lowther as vice president and J. Lee Harne as cashier, who are the present officers. The capital is $50,000. The directors are S. B. Hall, J. W. Kauffman, H. R. Thompson, A. E. McCaskey, A. C. Ruby, Robert Morris, R. C. Leap, .F P. Lowther, F. F. Morgan, A. T. Fair, Amos Joliffe, W. M. Garner, J. R. Parr, Felix Abersold and T. M. Jackson.

SMITHFIELD BANK.

Is located at Smithfield. I. D. Morgan is president and W. A. Lewis is cashier. The capital stock is $25,000.00.

BANK OF LITTLETON

Opened June 1st, 1901, with J. A. Connelly as president and B. A. Pyles as cashier, and has a capital stock of $25.000.

CHURCHES OF NEW MARTINSVILLE.

METHODIST EPISCOPAL CHURCH.

Meetings of this church were held many years prior to the building of the meeting house in the old court house and old school house. The old building was erected in 1854, under the pastorate of Rev. J. J. Dolliver, who was succeeded by Rev. Wm. Williamson. Rev. G. D. Smith is the present incumbent. A very beautiful church building was erected in 1901 by the members of the church under the supervision of Rev. Smith, who is constituted an efficient worker.

METHODIST EPISCOPAL CHURCH (SOUTH.)

Rev. G. B. Page was the pioneer Methodist preacher, who came here in the year of 1856, and was followed by Rev. C. M. Sullivan, of the Parkersburg district, who preached occasionally, when he could get off from his other work. After the meeting of the general conference in New Orleans in the year of 1866, Rev. R. A. Claughton re-established the church here. He was succeeded by Rev. E. Kendal. Rev. Gosling is the present incumbent.

ST. ANNE'S EPISCOPAL CHURCRH.

This church was organized at New Martinsville in the year of 1881, when Rev. A. Buchanan was appointed minister. He was succeeded by Rev. I. Brittingham. The present minister is Rev. Burkhardt.

THE CHRISTIAN CHURCH.

This church was organized in the year of   and has continued to grow from its organization. The present minister is Rev. Light.

THE CATHOLIC CHURCH.

The Catholic Church was organized in the year of 1865.

NEWSPAPERS OF WETZEL.

The first paper issued in Wetzel county was issued by Daniel Long, in 1870, under the name of the "Wetzel Independent," and published at New Martinsville. In 1872 Mr. Long changed its name to the Labor Vindicator, and continued its publication until 1876, when it was suspended. After a short time the name of the paper was taken up by W. W. Roberts and published at Hundred, with W. W. Roberts as editor, until 1900, when he died, and the paper is now owned and edited by his son, C. W. Roberts.

The Wetzel Democrat was issued in 1877 with W. S. Wiley and Robert McEldowney as editors, and Dan Long as publisher. The editorial management remained the same until 1900, when Colonel McEldowney died. The paper then came into the hands of C. C. Westerman, who is the present editor and publisher.

The Messenger was published at New Martinsville in 1876 by J. E. Hart. It was afterwards purchased by E. E. Eisenbarth, with T. P. Jacobs as editor. It was then transferred back to Hart, who published it under the name of the Wetzel Republican. The present publishers are Smith & Fitch. The present editor is Robert Smith.

The Smithfield Derrick is published at Smithfield. It was not issued until 1901. Mrs. R. C. Walker is publisher and R. C. Walker is editor.

The New Martinsville News is a new paper published by a number of Wetzel county citizens.

THE JENNINGS GANG.

A book was written in 1874 on the Jennings gang, but of course contains a great deal of fiction, to make a book of its size, although it was based on facts; and the writer by many has been accused of being one of the gang, and it is a fact that he served two terms in the penitentiary for forgery. Whether John Jennnigs was the chief of the Jennings gang, as has been stated, I will leave it to the reader to decide. It is said that he at one time ordered Jack away from the house, upon which he was shot upon by him, and merely escaped with his life. They often had long combats, in which he would beat his father up wonderfully, and when the old man would get on top of him, he would hallow that he was killing him. That shows what an inhuman creature he was, and we shall describe him later as one of the gang and the most treacherous of their number.

JOHN JENNINGS.

We will first give the life of John Jennings. He was a native of Monongalia county, W. Va., and at the time of his death was fifty-two years of age. He bore the reputation of being an honest man, up to the time of the civil war. When the war broke out he took very ardent sides with the Union cause, and denounced with bitterness the principles of secession. He enlisted in the 15th W. Va. infantry, and remained in the service but six months, when his devotion for his wife and children, made him desert his regiment and come home. But he had no more than got home, when he found that he had been followed by a military officer, with a company of soldiers. He succeeded in escaping them. Squads of men were sent, from time to time, with instructions to arrest him, but he always succeeded in escaping. He knew the hills of Wetzel county as well as he knew the hills around the old homestead, and could easily escape hundreds of men. He also had so many relations throughout the locality which was searched, that it was almost impossible to secure his arrest. Owing to the determination of the military authorities to capture him, he was compelled to abandon the comforts of home, and become a wanderer, and sleep in the woods, or at the home of a near relative. Hunted from one place to another by squads of soldiery, he began to be looked on by many as an outlaw. When he was about to be driven into desperation by the home guards President Lincoln came to his rescue, and issued a pardon to all deserters, who would come back to their respective regiments. He at once rejoined his regiment, and, it is said, was treated like a dog by his comrades. They would not speak to him, only in a commanding way, and would make him set his tent off by itself, when in camp. On the way home, after the disbandment of the army, he was forcibly seized, and thrown overboard of the steamer that was carrying them home. He was then compelled to walk to his destination. He was twice married, both of his wives being good, respectable women, and devoted to their husband. His first wife died, it is alleged, from exposure and fatigue, incurred by her in carrying him food and clothing while he was a fugitive. After he had been discharged from the service of the government, he married one Mrs. Sallie Huff, a woman of good reputation, and of considerable intelligence, who was devoted to him during his long and weary trials. He had by his first wife nine children, five sons and four daughters. All his sons, except one, who was called little John, and William, who was drowned accidentally long before the gang broke out, were members of the gang, and on or before that John Jennings was one of our best citizens and was often selected as a juryman. One of the girls married Alfred Spicer, a respectable farmer and good citizen, living in this county. One of the other girls was less fortunate, eloping

with a married man.   Jennings was a man of energy, courage
and indomitable will, and a man who would sacrifice anything
necessary for a friend, but who would shoot down whom he
considered his enemy as he would a dog.   His residence, which
was the headquarters of the gang, was situated in a quiet
place between two streams, Dulin and Big Fishing creek.   It
was situated on an isolated piece of ground some distance from
the main road, surrounded with heavy timber and dense under-
brush.   The woods contained secret paths, known only to the
members of the gang.   If John Jennings was not the chief of
the Jennings gang he harbored them, as most fathers would
have done, when it came to the time of driving them away from
home.   It will be impossible to give a life of all of the members of the gang, but of those whom were known to be members of the gang, we will first give a sketch of Frank Jennings.

FRANK JENNINGS.

One of the most desperate and reckless criminals the State
has ever been cursed with, says Stienmetz, in his sketch of
him.   He was a young man not more than twenty-four years
of age.   No less than a half dozen, if not more, have been spent
in criminal pursuits.   He had little intelligence, and a common school education.   Tall, strong and athletic, of a pleasant
expression; he was as straight as an Indian, and was the most
feared of the gang when a boy.   He bore the reputation of a
dare devil, but nothing criminal was imputed by him until the years of 1864-65.   He did more criminal business than
did any other member of the gang, with the exception of
Benjamin Barcus.   He was in all of the deeds committed by
the gang, but was charged of but one, on which he was sentenced to five years in the penitentiary at Moundsville, but
succeeded in escaping before more than one-half of his term
was out.   His daring recklessness was shown on that occasion.
The building of the penitentiary was not completed yet, and
the walls of the same were inclosed by a stockade of two-inch

plank, sixteen feet high. A sentry box was erected on each side of the stockade; in each of these a guard was placed, who was armed with a seven shooter. This stockade, having been exposed for a number of years, was beginning to decay. On one occasion a severe rain storm, followed by a violent wind, was seen approaching, and the guards were beginning to fear that the stockade would fall down, and that was all that stood between over one hundred convicts, and many of them fearless desperadoes. These convicts knew that they were to face the seven shooters, and freedom was their own. As the storm neared them they gathered in groups discussing plans of escape. All eyes were turned toward Frank Jennings, as their leader. Not since the death of Woodford L. Crews had the penitentiary received a more daring criminal than Frank Jennings. He willingly consented, but they must swear to follow him. He knew that many would, when the trying moment came, fail. He knew that he could rely upon but a few, if any. But he told them that as soon as the stockade fell that a rush must be made, and that no regard must be paid for orders, and not to pay any attention to their seven-shooters. All consented and professed eagerness to follow, and congregated under one of the large sheds in the yard, anxiously waiting the coming storm. The officers saw the movements of the men and knew what those movements meant, and stationed all of the men they could spare at that place. The storm came on and raged with terrible fury, the rain falling in torrents, and the wind blowing a perfect gale. The decaying stockade trembled and swung back and forth, eagerly watched by guards and officers without and by a band of excited convicts within. Yielding to the force of the tornado, it at last fell with a crash, and the barrier between them and liberty was down. With a shout, a rush was made, Frank Jennings at the head of the column. They were valiently met by the little squad of guards armed with carbines and ordered to halt and desist. Not heeding their admonitions, they continued to advance and the guards were compelled to fire. Every man halted and turned back save one, and that was Frank Jennings. Running at the top of his speed, he cleared the fallen timbers at a bound, regardless of the shouts and threats of the guards, and though half a dozen shots were fired at him, he succeeded in effecting his escape, and in forty-eight hours was received with open arms at the headquarters of the gang, but he did not remain there, for he knew that officers would be after him in a few hours. His confederates had a score of hiding places for him, and he well knew where he would be safe. In the course of a few days two of the officers of the penitentiary came to New Martinsville and engaged the services of several citizens to aid them in their efforts to capture Frank Jennings. They waited patiently until after dark before they made known the nature of their visit, or before they undertook to solicit the services of others, thinking that they would succeed in locating his retreat and capture him without difficulty. Foolish men! Their arrival had been expected long before they left the county seat. Frank had been informed of the fact, and of their plans and intentions. The spies of the gang were near them, conversing with them, denouncing the course of Frank Jennings and all who bore the name, and then they told tales of how much danger there was in seeking such men; that Coal Run was especially unsafe; that the villains would be within four feet of the road, shoot down the officers in the darkness and effect their escape. So misled, deceived and terrified were they, that they actually returned to Moundsville without having accomplished their object; in fact, without attempting it. So this ended the chase after Frank Jennings. He remained in the county unmolested until the death of his father. He did not at all times keep himself concealed. He was frequently seen on the Doolin road and scores of times escaped from his father's house by secret paths, to the opposite side of the hills, among his friends. The next thing would be news of his robbing a house or some other crime. A portion of the time his retreat was in a small cabin, from which he had an outlook in every direction, with a subterranean passage of nearly two hundred yards, ending in a ravine, from which he could escape in any direction. The entrance to the underground channel was effected by raising a board or plank in the floor, which, after descending, he could draw after him and securely fasten it to its original position. Should his foes even succeed in forcing their way into his cabin, which was impossible without loss of life, for he always was armed, he could be in the ravine long before they could discover his way of escape or explore the passage when once found. He could well adapt himself to his surroundings, and when necessary could easily put on the mask of hypocrisy and profess religion. None could be more devout than he; none could shout louder, sing more vigorously, or pray more earnestly, and such feeling addresses—how ungrateful he had been; but thank God, the scales have fallen from his eyes; he could now see how good God had been to him, and an hour later he could have been indulging in quite a different strain. He was no doubt the leader of the gang, and was always on the alert.

THOMAS JENNINGS.

There is another of that family in the gang worthy of mention. It is Frank's brother, Thomas Jennings. He was older than his brother Frank. He became about as notorious as the other members, but probably his notoriety was to be attributed largely to his connection to the Jennings family, more than his criminal exploits. Like his father, he was not naturally a criminal, as were his other brothers. He was engaged in fewer criminal transactions than any other member of the gang. He was young, not being more than twenty-seven years of age at the time of his death, which occurred at the penitentiary hospital in 1872. Like his father, he entered the military service of the United States and deserted therefrom, but unlike his father, did not return to his regiment at the time of

Lincoln's proclamation. His most prominent action was in the shooting of Geo. Forbes, of Wheeling. He had been arrested and tried for grand larceny and sentenced to an imprisonment in the penitentiary, which term he served. He was not out of the prison twenty-four hours until he was among his old confederates in crime, and roamed the country with disreputable females, such as Beck Craig and Mollie Vanhorn, indulging in conduct so disgraceful as to be unfit for publication. He was again indicted with Rebecca J. Craig upon the charge of grand larceny, breaking into the house of one George Alter. For this he was sentenced to five years in the penitentiary. This sentence was terminated by his death, which occurred while there. A fearful epidemic was raging in the penitentiary, to which he fell a victim.

Thomas Jennings was so much like his brother Frank that there is no use to rewrite his history.

JACKSON JENNINGS.

There is another who was one of the most cruel and inhuman men that ever stood upon the soil of Wetzel county. His name is Jackson Jennings, commonly known as Jack Jennings. He was a brother to Thomas and Frank, and younger than either. He was the most unscrupulous member of that family. Like his brothers, he was ready at any time to commit a robbery. He was less intelligent than the others, and equally illiterate, without a redeeming trait about him. He was not capable of planning or carrying out any plan, as was Frank, without a leader, and it was necessary that he should act in a secondary capacity. Jack could not play the part of a hypocrit, as could Frank. While Frank would never betray a friend, Jack would for the sake of money, or for the purpose of escaping punishment. He would betray his best friend. For female virtue he had no respect whatever. The language that he has used in the presence of his own sisters and mother dare not be repeated here. He did not know what the sacred words of mother or sister meant. In this respect he was the opposite of his brother Thomas, and it is pleasant to the writer to bear this testimony in behalf of the latter. Jack Jennings was hostile toward his father, disliked to acknowledge his authority. On several occasions he threatened to take his father's life, and made an assault on him, and it was some time before the breach between the two was healed. So depraved was he that his father stood in fear of his personal safety, and on two occasions sought the aid and advice of the authorities, taking the necessary steps to have him arrested. It was at these times that people were beginning to think that the old man had nothing to do with the gang. He frequently stated that he had no control over him; that he would pay no attention to his orders or requests; that he would, contrary to parental wishes, bring to the house disreputable persons for him to lodge and feed, and that when he ventured to remonstrate the son would seize a revolver or rifle and threaten to terminate the old man's existence. He complained bitterly of the conduct of his son and frequently remarked that he was being accused of harboring bad men under his roof, when in fact, he was opposed to such proceedings, and would often warn his son not to repeat these offenses, but that he was only threatened with his life. He complained that it was hard that he should have the enmity and ill will of his neighbors for acts done by his son. But enough has been said of the ill-fated family, so I will give a sketch of the next member of the gang.

BENJAMIN BARCUS.

Benjamin Barcus was a native of Marshall county. It is extremely difficult to give the reader a correct and full sketch of him, says Steinmetz. In his life he managed to make himself notorious as a criminal. In early life he was afflicted with kleptomania, with an equine tendency. He frequently engaged in horse dealing of a peculiar nature. He would sometimes be seen traveling through the country as a peddler, sell-

ing dry goods at rates that would have been ruinous to ordinary retail dealers in dry goods, but not ruinous to him, having the good fortune to obtain his stock of goods without giving
any consideration. This was a slow way to make money in
Ben's eyes, and besides, it required labor to carry his pack
from one house to another. Dealing in counterfeit national
currency was an easy and genteel business, but where could he
get his material? To Ben this was a great difficulty. At last
he became acquainted with Frank, and Jack Jennings, and
they told him glowing tales of Wetzel, and how many families
were there who had money in their possession, and then the
country stores, filled with dry goods, with no person remaining in the building during the night; how easy to enter and
carry away with them the entire stock. Such glowing accounts did he receive of the many golden opportunities Wetzel
afforded such men that he concluded as soon as his time of imprisonment expired, to report for duty at the Jennings headquarters.

"Upon a warm summer day in the year of 1872, a rather tall
man, with brown hair and beard, gray eyes and an awkward
gait, passed the residence of Nelson Garner and inquired the
way of him to the residence of John Jennings, and received the
desired information." That man was Benjamin Barcus, just
discharged from prison, and then on his way to the headquarters of the Jennings gang. In less than thirty days thereafter
the breaking into of the house of and brutal assault upon John
Burrows, an old disabled citizen, by himself and Jack Jennings, proved how ready he was to begin his infamous work.
Like Frank Jennings he was possessed of a rare line of human
nature and could act the hypocrite to perfection, and was a
power at a meeting. He could shout, sing, pray and exort to
anything that was required in that line, except to the shedding
of tears. He could not quite adapt himself to that. He
served a term out in the Ohio penitentiary, upon which he was
convicted of a felony. He has also served two terms out in

the West Virginia penitentiary and was pardoned the first term by Governor Boreman, who was deceived by the representations made to him.

MOLLIE VANHORN.

Mollie Vanhorn, another member of the Jennings gang, has quite a history, and if published would create quite a sensation. Her history is still imperfectly known to the people at large. She was a woman of remarkable beauty and more than an ordinary share of intelligence, and her connection and acts with them must be deeply regretted. She was in point of intelligence and education the superior of many in the county, who would not tolerate her presence socially among them. She was capable of adapting herself to their surroundings. Her physical beauty was equalled by few in Wetzel county. Immorality was her first offense, and, of course, the downward path speedily followed. She was a niece of John Jennings, being an illegitimate daughter of his sister, Ortha, who afterward married one Nicholas Cross, a harmless and inoffensive man. Most people knew her reputed father, but it dare not be put in print. She was married to a man by the name of Vanhorn, who after their marriage entered the military service of the United States, and during his absence it was reported that she was guilty of adultery. Her mother-in-law witnessing these proceedings, wrote to her son and told him of her actions, and he immediately disowned her as a wife. There are people now who are thought to be respectable, and who have large families, who have spent whole nights with Mollie Vanhorn. She herself declared that there were those who claimed to be respectable and deemed themselves aristocratic, who were nevertheless, on very intimate terms with her, having traveled together in different localities as man and wife, and afterwards endeavored to effect her capture. At one time fifty dollars was offered for her arrest, but she always escaped the hunting parties. She was arrested with Thomas

Jennings at the time he was sent for a year to the penitentiary, but escaped trial. One of the things that always enabled her to escape trial is that she has been intimate with so many respectable men in Wetzel county, that if she once got on trial would disgrace them as well as their families. She kept going downward from time to time. She became as notorious as her cousins, the Jennings boys. After the breaking up of the Jennings gang she joined a house of ill fame at Pittsburg. She was married to one Frances Sheppard, a discharged soldier of the Union army. He was so unfortunate as to become involved in a fight with a German at Hannibal, O., in which the latter lost his life, and Sheppard was indicted and found guilty of manslaughter and sentenced to the Ohio penitentiary for ten years. He was pardoned, and notwithstanding Mollie's infamous actions, he went back to her and became reconciled, and lived with her for a long time. The last account the author had of her whereabouts, was at Sistersville, where she applied for a place of employment in a respectable family, in which she was hired, and upon being asked her name, she replied Mollie Vanhorn. She was immediately discharged. Thus is a life which could have been passed in happiness. With her beauty and refinement she could have been surrounded with everything that made life dear, and it was spent in misery and disgrace. Her last husband, Frank Sheppard, was not a man of bad reputation. He was not a member of the Jennings gang, but a hard working man, whose trouble originated from intoxication.

CHARLES CANNON.

But little is known of the next member of the gang, more than that he was known by the name of Charles Cannon, and was introduced to different parties by John Jennings as his nephew. He was convicted in one of the counties of West Virginia as Charles Willard, of grand larceny. He had a peculiar expression of countenance. He was ready at any time to do anything that was criminal. There was not a crime known that he was not ready at any time to commit. He claimed to have been a soldier in the federal army, and was at the battle of Pittsburg Landing, but was unable to give his organization. He was lame in walking, which he claimed was caused by a bullet shot which he received at the battle of Shiloh. He was fortunate enough at an early age to acquire a common school education, of which he frequently engaged in reading stories of noted highwaymen, such as Dick Turpin, Jack Sheppard and others. But little is known of his connection with the Jennings gang, more than that he was a member.

JIM PARKER.

There is still another member of the gang who is worthy of mention. That man was Jim Parker. This man is more noted in his connection with the shooting of Mr. Forbes, of Wheeling. He was pleasant and agreeable and one whose sociable manner would win the confidence of most anyone. Even in prison he was cheerful and obeyed prison orders, endeavoring to yield a pleasant and implicit obedience to the discipline of the prison. While serving his second term he openly denounced the Jennings boys, and claimed that he was now suffering for a crime that was committed by the Jennings boys, and both Frank and Tom said that he was not guilty. While the great revival was in progress, the officers were surprised to see such depraved as wretches as Frank Jennings and Luther Cremeens suddenly become converted. Parker was strongly urged to join in the movement by those who were making professions, for the purpose of fraud, but he bitterly denounced those whom he knew to be hypocrits. Among the number was Frank Jennings. He accused him of making those professions for the purpose of making the officers believe that he was going to do better, and thus escape the punishment he too often deserved. These actions on the part of Par-

ker made him honorable in the minds of the officers and he
gained the sympathy of those who came in contact with him.
It was believed by a number of people throughout Wetzel and
adjoining counties that he was innocent of the shooting of
Mr. Forbes, of Wheeling, and Parker said that he believed that
Forbes was honest in making his statement that he was the
man that shot him, and that he could not in the excitement of
such a thing identify his attempted murderer. It is believed
that his connection with the Jennings gang had more to do
with securing his conviction than Mr. Forbes' testimony.

LUTHER CREMEENS.

The next member of the gang is Luther Cremeens. Cremeens was a native of Kanawha county. He was one of the
worst dare-devils that West Virginia has ever produced. Ready
at any time to commit a crime (no matter how bad it was) for
the sake of money. He formed the acquaintance of the Jennings in the West Virginia penitentiary, as did most of the
members of the Jennings. He was convicted in Kanawha
county of manslaughter and sentenced to a term of ten years
in the State penitentiary. His first object when reaching
prison was to discover what opportunities were afforded for
escape, and watched closely, but he had not long to wait. On
the 22nd day of August, 1867, the inmates at that time being
allowed to purchase any luxuries that they were able to pay
for, and on the morning of that day groups of men were scattered here and there discussing plans of escape. At their
head were J. L. Graham, Chester Crawford and Luther Cremeens, and on that morning Graham arose as he had done
numbers of times before and started toward the gate with a
small tin bucket. Knocking on the gate it was opened by the
keeper. Graham then told him that he wanted some milk, on
which the keeper took the bucket and started after it, holding
the bucket in one hand and trying to shut the gate in the other.
At that moment Graham suddenly swung back the gate and

shouted: "Come on, boys, if you want your liberty!" Out marched twenty-seven men, who seized the arms of the guard and compelled them to surrender, and marched in good order toward the hills, with Luther Cremeens at their head. For a long time Cremeens remained at large and what crimes he committed during that time are not known. He was again captured and taken back to prison and succeeded in affecting his escape in 1868, and it was while he was in the second time that he became acquainted with the Jennings boys, but he was with them but a short time when he was again captured and taken back to prison. He was captured the last time by Thomas H. Snodgrass.

FRANK GODDARD.

We will not introduce a new character, well known to the people, Frank Goddard. None of the Jennings gang was more despised than he by the people of Wetzel county. He was not a thief or robber, but a spy, and gave the necessary evidence in court needed by the defence in the trials of the Jennings boys. He would visit the prosecuting attorney's office and try to find out the mode of proceedure in the capturing of the Jennings gang, and would often denounce the Jennings boys for the purpose of securing something that might prove useful to them. There was a difficulty in proving his connection with the Jennings gang, but it was evident that he was a member. It is also evident that he received money for his services, for he had a family to keep, who were provided for. Yet he never worked.

REASON GODDARD.

We will now introduce to the reader Frank Goddard's son, Reason Goddard. This man did little actual service for them. He was too cowardly and worthless, says Steinmetz, who, if all reports were true, ought to know. He was one who bore dispatches and, like his father, a spy. His stealing, if any was done, was on his own responsibility, and of a petty order. There is no use taking up the space in this book speaking of such a worthless character.

JAMES BERRY.

There is another who should not be overlooked, James Berry. His house was often visited by the Jennings gang, and was used by them as one of their headquarters. His home was the stopping place for disreputable women. It was the headquar- ters of the notorious Susan Hopkinson. She was the most in- famous of her sex in the country, and it is to be regretted that the term of woman can be applied to such a creature. She was so abandoned and so utterly lost to every sense of the word that sympathy was beyond her reach. Among the Jennings gang she was the almost constant companion of Cannon, and the whole house of Berry was a rendezvous of a lot of women whose honor had gone beyond recall, and those who were in- timate with the members of the Jennings gang, such as Beck Craig and Mollie Vanhorn. The latter cannot by any ways be compared with Susan Hopkinson. Though Mollie could have been respected, it is doubtful if the former could ever have been. Had it not been for the aid that Berry received from the gang, he would have hardly been able to support his family.

REBECCA J. CRAIG.

Another disreputable female who was connected with the gang was Rebecca J. Craig, familiarly known as Beck Craig. She was as abandoned as was Susan Hopkinson, but while the latter escaped indictment for a felony, Beck did not, there being for a long time on file at the clerk's office an indictment for grand larceny. She was for a while the constant companion of Thomas Jennings, and roamed with him night and day, camping in the woods and preying upon peaceable and unof- fending citzens and committing crimes more annoying than criminal. Not being satisfied with operating on so small a scale they committed a crime more serious, on which both were indicted, and Thomas convicted and sent to the penitentiary. After his conviction he was succeeded by Frank and Jack Jennings, while after their conviction, Reason Goddard, abandoning his wife and children, would accompany her; but we will now leave her to give a sketch of one who was thought to be one of the gang.

FREEMAN WHIPKY.

Freeman Whipky, was a brother-in-law to John Jennings. His principal offense in the eyes of the people was harboring the gang and securing such information as they might need He was not recognized by the people as a good citizen. He was addicted to drinking and gambling, harboring women of ill fame and occasionally made a visit to a near neighbor's smoke house.

HENRY GODDARD.

There is still another member of the gang of considerable importance. This was Henry Goddard; whether a relative of Frank it is not known by the author, but it is probable that he was. He was a natural born thief, and a man without honor or conscience. He would steal the last cent from those who had gained it by charity. His wife was equally as bad. They would often steal from those who had done them a favor. They richly deserved the fate so nearly meted out from the hands of the red men.

There is another member of the gang, who if a description were given, it would be a repetition of the sketch just given of Henry Goddard. Jerry Bondine was a neighbor of Henry Goddard, and between the families, in their low and petty crimes, it is difficult to find a difference.

There is still another member, and the last we shall mention, as there are a number of families through the county who were connected with the gang through fear, and probably some we have mentioned were connected with them with the same ex-cuse. It may be we have spoken too harshly of them, but we will now take up the sketch of the last man we shall mention,

FRANK JACKSON.

Frank Jackson, alias Burns. It is not probable that Burns or Jackson, ever had the opportunity of participating in any of the serious offences committed by the gang. He was a native of Virginia (not West Virginia). He was convicted of larceny and sent to the penitentiary, where he served his time, and was again sent to the same place and made his escape with Luther Cremeens. Like the latter, was captured by Thos. H. Shep-pard and James Sheppard and taken back to prison, where he remained until not long ago, after which it is thought that he concluded to seek an honest livelihood.

CRIMES COMMITTED BY THE GANG.

We will not dwell largely upon the crimes committed by the gang more than to mention them. The first crime known was the robbing of one Nicholas Hitch, who owned a store in the place known as Stender's. Another outrage committed by the gang was the shooting of one George Forbes, a cattle dealer, of Wheeling, in which he was wounded severely and laid for a long time with the wound he had received. The robbing of Stephen Howell was another outrage committed by the gang. The robbing of Lemaster's store, in Tyler county, also the rob-bing of John Burrows, John Clark, Mr. Grossenbaucher, Mr. Bucherm, and others too numerous to mention. Nearly all of the members of the gang had served terms in the penitentiary, and at one time very near all of the gang, yet outrages were still committed. The people by this time were trying every way to find means of breaking up the gang, but could accom-plish nothing. At last a secret organization was formed under the name of the Redmen, and these men determined to stop what the law so far had failed to do. Jennings was warned of the storm that was near by a piece published in the Labor Vindicator, and it was Jennings' own obstinate ways that shortened his life. On the night of June 12th, 1873, while lying in bed at his home in slumber, and little dreaming that that night would be his last on earth, he was awakened by a shot, doubtless fired at the faithful watch dog, and on looking out beheld the members of the Redmen, who were more than a score in number, and their faces painted with red paint. He at once knew what it meant. He was no coward, but when he thought of his past life and of the widow and the youngest son, his limbs began to tremble, but he was going to face death like a man. He was ordered to surrender. This, of course, he refused to do. He was then commanded to follow them, and again he refused. An attempt was then made to fasten a rope around his neck. His wife seeing this, and knowing the meaning, handed him an axe, on which Jennings was shot by one of the Redmen and fell lifeless to the floor. His wife also received two bullet wounds, though testifying before the coroner's jury that she did not believe the shots were intended for her. She afterward remarked that she believed they were. It is the opinion of the writer that they were not thus intended. The Jennings gang, Jack and Frank, were in the South the last time they were heard of, but the other members of the gang disappeared, as did the Jennings boys, and not since then, with but one exception, has there ever been a person unlawfully hung or shot by a mob.

THE GHOST OF GAMBLE'S RUN.

This article is not based upon superstition, but it is written to show one of the peculiar cases that has been in the courts, since the formation of the county. The following sketch was written by D. W. Gamble, who was then but ten years old, but who remembers the incident very well, it being revised and corrected by the author.

John Gamble, of whom our story relates, was born in Beaver county, Pennsylvania, in the year of 1814. He was a house carpenter by trade, and helped build the second house built in New Cumberland. In the year of 1850, he moved on the farm now owned by the D. W. Skinner heirs, near Sardis Station, on the West Virginia side. He often engaged in buying up staves, tanbark and wagon spokes, and carried them down the Ohio river in flat boats to Cincinnati. The same year he moved to this county there was a very large crop of apples, there being two large orchards on the farm he moved on, and one of the orchards contained crab apples. He went to work, and with hired help, made a number of barrels of cider, and on the afternoon of November 12th, same year, it being the thirty-sixth anniversary of his birth, he started from home in a hurry for New Martinsville, with a skiff, after barrels to put the rest of his cider in, but he never returned, for that very night he was murdered by one Leb Mercer. Now to bring about the facts of the deed. The writer was about ten years old, at the time, and well remembers the incident. John Gamble had a wagon, and sold it to the Whiteman Brothers, who then lived on what was then the Cox farm, and now the property of the Short Line Railroad Company and the heirs of John R. Brown, and took their note for twenty dollars, and after going to New

Martinsville, on his return he stopped at the home of the Whiteman Brothers, where he asked the boys if they wanted to cash the note, on which they remarked that they did not. He put it back in his pocket. John Gamble also dealt in cattle, and some time previous to this occasion, had purchased a calf from Mercer, on which he paid him all but two dollars. On meeting him at the home of the Whiteman Brothers, Mercer asked him for the money, upon which Gamble drew from his pocket a five dollar bill, and asked him if he had change for that, and Mercer replied that he had not. Mercer then asked him if that was all he had, and he said no. That he had something near two hundred dollars. It was now beginning to get dark, and Gamble started for home, and told Mercer to come to his house in a few days and he would pay him. Mercer then stood watching him, and after Gamble had got in his skiff and pushed it out into the river, Mercer started toward him. That night he came home about two o'clock, wet and muddy. The evidence was sorely against him, though he presented the note that the Whiteman brothers had given to Gamble for payment. The thing now laid over for a year, and in the fall of 1851 there was a cornhusking near Point Pleasant ridge, and a number of people from New Martinsville attended. Among them was one John Hindman. On their return home they decided to all go different routes and see who got there first. Hindman took over the hill, coming over what is now known as Gamble's run (so named from Gamble), and as he was walking along a path which was then on the river bank, he saw the form of a man, who remarked: "I am John Gamble; Leb Mercer killed me. Take him up and have justice done," and suddenly disappeared from view. Hindman being very badly scared, walked rapidly toward town, and the next morning told what he had seen. It was not believed by many people. Though he had never seen Gamble, he described his walk, clothes, etc. Mercer was arrested for murder in the first degree, which under the old law meant death or freedom, and he was released on the

grounds that ghost evidence would not go in court.   It was believed by many that he was guilty of the crime, and it is said
that his lawyer had a very hard time to keep him from con-
fessing the crime.   He is now living back of St. Marys, W Va.
where it is said he acts very strangely, often muttering to himself.

BIRDSEYE VIEW OF NEW MARTINSVILLE, FROM MARKER'S HILL IN 1891.

A HISTORY OF NEW MARTINSVILLE.

Edward Doolin, Its First Settler, Killed by the Indians on the Present
Site of the Town—Some Interesting Facts Not Generally Known
by the Present Generation.

About the year 1780, Edward Doolin patented and made entry upon 800 acres of Ohio river hill and bottom land, which included in its boundaries the present site of the town of New Martinsville. The piece of land was a little more than a mile square, and lay in the angle formed by Fishing creek and the Ohio river. He cleared some land and built a small cabin near where now stands the Witten dwelling, selecting that spot on account of its nearness to a spring, it being the source of little Doolin, which runs through town. He farmed and improved on his land until 1784.

In September of that year a small band of Indians came down the river from the village of Wheeling, where they had been driven off by Colonel Zane attacked his home unawares, and killed him. His wife and one child escaped. She retained ownership of the property for a time, selling it piece by piece.

The portion upon which the town is situated, was purchased by Presly Martin, the man for whom New Martinsville was named. Mr. Martin came here in 1811. He built a part of what is now the Point House, and planted an orchard of five acres between Washington street and the creek; a few trees are yet standing. Five years later he was followed by Friend Cox, who took up a farm and erected a house below the creek, opposite the Point House. This house has recently burned down.

From this time until 1838 the settlement grew slowly. On March 28th of that year an act establishing the town of "Martinsville," in the county of Tyler, was passed by the Assembly of Virginia, and in the same act Henry McCabe, Samuel McEldowney, Lewis Williams, John Buchanon and Benjamin F. Martin were appointed trustees to administer the affairs of the town. The surveying and platting was done by Lewis Williams and three others. It extended from one lot below Washington street to North street, and from Union street to the river. The streets included in these boundaries remain the same now as then, except Water street. This street was located on the river bank and was the widest and principal street in town, being 80 feet wide. It is evident that it was the purpose of the founders of this town to have a broad street on the river front, where they could have the benefit of the cool breezes from the west, and an open view of the river. I imagine that trees had been left along the bank for the purpose of shade, and that the residents had placed benches under there, where the gentry were accustomed to loaf and discuss the issues of the day. I am informed that in 1842 there were twelve houses in town.

An incident occurred in 1845 that must have aroused dreams of wealth. A man presented himself to the community and remained awhile without any apparent means of support. Having no occupation, he was arrested under the vagrancy law, and to obtain his liberty was compelled to state his business to the town officers. Thereupon he showed papers from the French Government. By this it was ascertained that he was an accredited agent of that government sent to this community to search for $87,000.00 supposed to have been buried below the creek during the French and Indian war. It is thought that he did not find the money. Shortly after this, another incident occurred in the same line. A Mr. Watkins

THE EAKIN HOUSE,
Better Known as the old Wetzel House
Justus Eakin, Proprietor.

BRAST HOUSE,
At New Martinsville,
Mike, Amos and Jacob Brast, Props.

of Monongalia county sold his farm there for 1,000 silver dollars, and came to this settlement; the silver, which weighed over 60 pounds, was too heavy to carry about his person, so he set aside $40.00 for his immediate use, and buried the remainder at the foot of a paw paw bush, 60 steps from the river bank, midway between the mouth of the creek and a point opposite Texas run; when he returned for his money, it could not be found.

An act prescribing the mode of electing trustees of New Martinsville in the county of Wetzel, and investing them with certain corporate powers was passed March 13th, 1848, by the Assembly of Virginia.

These trustees were elected annually by the people. They chose out of their own number to preside at their meetings. The subordinate officers were: Commissioner of Revenue, Sergeant or Town Collector and Police.

At this time also, the town was extended to the creek, and the McClure addition on High street taken in. The new part of the town was surveyed and marked out by Thomas Tucker, who died several years ago.

Observe that the town was called "Martinsville in Tyler county." Now it is called, "New Martinsville in Wetzel county," Wetzel having been carved out of the North end of Tyler county in 1846.

The first County Court of Wetzel county was held April 6th, 1846. The justices present were Sampson Thistle, Friend Cox. William Little and Ebenezer Payne. Presley Martin was elected first Clerk, and James Snodgrass first Prosecuting Attorney.

During the last decade, quite a number of well known names of the past and present moved to the burg: Houblers, the Villers, the Biers, the Wises, the Halls, Snodgrasses, the Pottses. the Livelys, the Tuckers, the Coulters, the Moores, the Pitchers and the Vances.

As the town was increasing in size and business, some of the

more active spirits desired to make a better connection with
the outside world, and accordingly, on the 21st day of February, 1853, the Mannington and New Martinsville railroad was
incorporated. The Directors were: Jas. G. West, Friend Cox,
Presley Martin, Joseph C. Moore, Robert Cox, Samuel McEldowney, George W. Bier, Joseph Vance, Edmund Moore, David
Cunningham, William P. Snodgrass, Elias Blackshire and
John Michael. If this railroad had been built, New Martinsville would probably be now where Wheeling is, or at least
much better off than she is.

The brick church that stood on Main street was built by the
Methodists in 1854. About the same time an Episcopal church
was built near this. It was sold and used for a school under
the name of the New Martinsville Academy. When the Free
School System was adopted by the State the building was used
for a public school. It was finally sold to Standiford Bros.,
who have erected a three story building on the old site.

The town was divided on the Civil War question, and during
that time many serious disturbances occurred and some of
them were amusing. There was one incident that caused consternation in the minds of many. A United States flag was
hung across Washington street for the purpose of proving the
loyalty of the citizens, by compelling them to walk under it.
One night was given to think over it, and all who would refuse
would do so at the peril of their lives. It was seen on the
morning of the fateful day, that the flag had disappeared, having been stolen during the night. The person who took it has
kept his secret.

After the war, the town made very little progress until 1871.
February 13th of that year, the Charter was amended and re-enacted bv the Legislature of West Virginia. From this time
onward, the town grew and improved more rapidly.

The Pittsburgh Stave Company came in 1873, and gave employment to 125 men.

In 1891 the Wetzel County Fair Association was organized

BIRDSEYE VIEW OF NEW MARTINSVILLE,
From the Ohio Side in 1894.

at that place and leased the ground here in the town where the Fair was and is now held. The next year Burlington sprang up, Eseec, John and Thomas Burlingame being the settlers. Springertown started up five years later. The school house was built in 1880. In 1882 a church boom struck the town, and the M. E. church South, P. E., Baptist, and Catholic churches were erected. The Ohio River Railroad was built in 1883.. In 1884 a flood came and was very destructive. The Clark and Martin's additions came later. The latest additions are Martin Burlingame, Clark, Stender and McEldowney. A boom struck the town in the last five years, on which the Short Line Railroad was built and the contracts for the erection of a new Court House and the new M. E. church let. The town has been booming for the past five years, and since that time a great many business houses and manufactories and fine resideuces have been built. The town has six churches, the two M. E. churches, the Catholic, Christian, Presbyterian and Episcopal; two school houses, one magnificent building which is being built by Contractor Burhart, six ladies' and gents' furnishing goods and shoe houses. They are Economy, Clarence Buhlingame, the Baltimore bargain house, Duerr Bros., John F. Loehr and J. M. Bender, and one in Brooklyn, The town has eight dry goods and notion stores, owned by Josephus Clark, Welch and Koontz, Mont Francis, Williams and Ankrom, N. Bandi, Levi Oblinger, Jacob Blair, Mont Burrows, Mr. Clark & Oblinger also have a hardware department to their store. Mr. Friend Wells and Bridgemen & Sons also have a hardware store. Seven groceries, Neff Bros. the Up-to-Date grocery, Geo. Rankin, who also keeps a full line of groceries and green goods. Mrs. Newton, who also deals in ice cream. Gorbey Bros., who keep a full line of groceries. Jacob Dennis, who also has a bakery, Mrs. G. Snodgrass and Smittle and Dunn. Three tailor shops owned by Geo. Grall, Duerr Bros. and D. C. Weatherhead. There are three drug stores, owned by R. T. Richardson, Dr. P. F. Lowther and P. D.

Leap; one laundry, owned by R. Dayton; two bakeries, owned by Irven Ober and Jacob Dennis; three millinery stores, owned by Mrs. S. M. Snodgrass, L. Pemberton, H. Hathaway, and four barber shops owned by Jacob Koontz, M. L. Kendal, Geo. Houdenshilt and Soland and Van Camp. Two jewelry stores, owned by Duerr Bros. and C. M. Powers. One harness shop owned by Dave Mangold; one tin shop owned by M. B. Potts and Mr. Owens; two plumber shops owned by Dewey Potts and M. F. Powers; two flour mills owned by Stender & Stamm, and John Nusum; four hotels, the Eakin, Brast, Elk and Wells; three restaurants, owned by Thompson, Patsey Finerty and Martin F. Williamson. The town is supplied with gas and water. Mack Snodgrass tends to the pump station. Wm. Fitch is superintendent of the gas office. There are two ice plants, one owned by the citizens of the town and the other by Schmulbach Brewing Company, of Wheeling. The glass house is another large concern, owned chiefly by the citizens. The wholesale grocery is a large business house, situated on Maple avenue. Robert Morris is manager. The town has two storage houses, owned by the Reymann and Schmulbach Brewing Companies, of Wheeling; two large livery barns, owned by A. C. Ruby and J. H. Bowen; three blacksmith shops, owned by Frank McEldowney, Glen Barrick and Geo. Harman. The town has six doctors, Drs. Schmied, Boone, Browse, Downing, Lowther and Grim. Sixteen lawyers, J. W. and L. V. McIntire, Brnice, Wm. McG. and Charles Hall, P. D. and Thomas Morris, S. B. McEldowney, Thos. H. Cornet, J. W. Newman, Mr. Morris, W. T. Sidel, T. P. Jacobs, E. B. Snodgrass, E. L. Robinson. R. E. L. Snodgrass, Thos. Mills, Bud Snodgrass and Frank Wells Clark. The present officers of the town are: Mayor, G. C. Westerman; Recorder, Jas. Bishop; Assessor, L. V. McIntire· Tax Collector, A. B. Morrison; Street Commissioner, vacant; Chief of Police, Ed. Luikhart. The councilmen for the First, Second and Third wards are Irven Ober, Jacob Koontz, A. C. Ruby, Wm. Culp, W. R. Rine and John Stender. Among the

EPISCOPAL CHURCH.
New Martinsville.

prosperous farmers around the town are John Stender John C. McEldowney, Duerr Brothers Owen and John Witten, Ben Bridgeman Josephus Clark Evan Williams John Cochran, Isaac Black, John Stephens, Mr. Linager, Brown Brothers, Mr. Bowman, Samuel Martin Felix Abersold Cris Anthony Gaberial Leap and Geo. Walker.

MORGANTOWN OR PORTER FALLS.

It was settled in 1818 by Morgan Morgan, better known as Paddy Mod; it was to distinguish him from his cousin by the same name who went by the name of Spy Mod. The town is situated in Green district, ten miles east of the county seat, on Big Fishing Creek, and the Short Line Railroad. It has about fifty inhabitants. The places of business in the town are: one store owned by Elsworth Sneider; one blacksmith shop, owned by George Midcap; and one saw mill owned by Morgan Bros., sons of Elisha Morgan. Morgan Morgan is postmaster. Among the prosperous farmers amound the town are Morgan Morgan Mrs. Jerry Long, Morgan Brothers, Lewis Kocher, Samuel Headlee, Z. Cochran, Aaron Morgan, William and Leonard Morgan.

OHIO RIVER RAILROAD DEPOT,
New Martinsville.

MINNIE.

Was settled in 1815 by Aaron Morgan, cousin of the noted Indian scout, Levi Morgan, and brother of Paddy Mod, the first settler in Porter's Falls. It is situated in Green district, six miles east of New Martinsville, the county seat, on the short line railroad and Big Fishing creek. The only place of business is a store owned by Reuben Yoho, who is also postmaster. Among the prosperous farmers around the postoffice are Ruben Yoho, Joe Wells, S. L. Morgan, Mrs. Aaron Clepstein Friend Wells, Richard Morgan, Jacob Shamp, John Shamp, Walter and Fred Shamp.

MONEY POSTOFFICE.

Is a post office situated on a small run by the same name, which enters into Big Fishing creek one mile west of Reader. It took its name from Money Bates, who located the land near the stream at an early date. Part of the survey is now owned by Ed. Winning, Charles Kiger, Ruben Price, Fred Grocenbaucher, John King, Wm. Mayhall, Geo. Brown, Isaac Smith, Albert Koch, Thomas McCalaster, John Stealey, James Windland, Charles Hudson, Wm. Gadd, Rosella Fiece, Wilson Furbee, Jason Furbee, John and James Furbee, Geo. Worth, J. L. Higgins, Elisha Barker, Geo. Garrett, R. Wright, Wm. Workman, Isaac Wright, John, David and Wm. Lancaster, N. Strait, Susan Blackbridge, Dr. John Garrett, Jake Haught, Alex. Strait, Dr. Parks, Andrew McHenry, Milton, Hiram and George Strait, James Kerby, Jackson Strait, Jenkins Miller William, Ulesses and Mack Miller.

OLD M. E. CHURCH. NORTH.

LOT

Is a town situated twenty-three miles east of the county seat. It has a population of about 340, and is rapidly growing, having the prospect of making one of the best towns along the Short Line Railroad. It was settled in the year of 1805 by James Hays, who came to that place and erected a cabin on the ground now owned by his grandson, G. T. Anderson. Other early settlers around the town were Jasper Wyatt, James Wiley, Alexander Lantz, H. King, Abraham Ice, and Aiden Bales. The town is favored with one of the best hotels along the Short Line Railroad between New Martinsville and Clarksburg. It is owned by W. A. Dye. There is one restaurant, owned by Mr. West; one drug store, owned by Dr's. McGriven and Clellan; three dry goods and notions stores, owned by Smith & Fitcher; L. E. Lantz and Lee Schrachfield; one confectionery store, owned by Mr. Harness; one bakery owned by Wm. Laudenslyn; one meat market, H. Taylor, proprietor; one blacksmith shop, owned by The. Y. Barrick; and one planing mill, owned by Curby & Mansfield. It has one church and one schoolhouse. Among the prosperous farmers around the town are Levi, John, Amos and Polk Lowe, Sam. Lantz, Alex Bluty, J. M. Anderson, Catherine Satterfield, Mary Cunningham, Thomas Gorby, J. R. Davis, Milton Anderson, J. M. Loveall, John Wiley, A. Wyatt, H. H. King, J. Markindle, Wm. Batson, Y. T. Frances, M. Wiley, Ed. Cain, Wm. Henthorn, Ezra Hays, Geo. Hickmon, Geo. Wetzel, L. and D. McIntire Elizabeth Morgan, Lot King and William Watson.

KODOL.

Is a postoffice situated in Wetzel county, lately organized. It was settled in the year 1854 by Silas J. Park, who came to that place and erected a house near the present site of the town of Kodol. It has three churches, Baptist, Methodist and Christian; and one school house. The postoffice was not organized until October, 1900, by J. J. Crawford, bodnsman and postmaster, and Stephen Park and I. N. Crawford. The town has two attorneys, F. Keller and E. Morris, and two doctors, Lemley and Cox. It has one store. The prosperous farmers around the town are Wm. Leaganden, I. C. Brookover, S. C. and S. W. Park and I. N. Crawford.

MAGNOLIA HIGH SCHOOL, OLD BUILDING.

SILVER HILL.

Is a village situated in Center district, It was settled in the year of 1825, by James A. Wood. The town has two churches, Christian and Methodist; one school house, two stores, owned by Rulong & Son, and C. E. Yeater; one blacksmith shop, owned by Geho & Harlan; one hotel, proprietor, W. J. Derrow. Among the prosperous farmers around the town are Wm. Car-ney, Solomon Carney, C. L. Yoho and S. C. Lowe.
L. Yoho and S. C. Lowe.

HAZEL

Is a postoffice in Grant district on Crow's run, twenty miles east of the county seat, and five miles south of Reader. Charles Fluharty is postmaster. The postoffice has one store and grist mill, both owned by Aaron Bassett. Among the prosperous farmers around the postoffice are Aaron Basset, James Martin, Lot Martin, Pleasance Myres, William Wright, Abraham Hiley, Charles Hiley, Friend Tracey, John Strait, Chas. Strait, E. M. Strait, Foster Higgins and Isaac Pitman.

F. W. PARSONS,
County Superintendent of Schools.

PINEY FORK.

Is neither a village nor a postoffice but a stopping place for a great many strangers. It is situated in Green district, on the Short Line Railroad, and twelve miles east of the county seat. It has one store and a hotel, both owned by Frank Stender.

MAUD.

Is a postoffice situated in Proctor district, ten miles from the county seat. It was settled in the year of 1801 by Gabrriel Leap, who came there and erected a cabin on the property now owned by Geo. W. Cook. The postoffice has one school house, one church, United Brethren, with W. W. Burgess as pastor; one lawyer, A. T. Morris. It has two stores, owned by F. P. Cook, who is also postmaster, and F. R. Suter. M .W. Burgess owns a sawmill. Joseph Burgess also owns a store and a blacksmith shop, Alexander Dulaney owns a gunsmith. Among the prosperous farmers around the postoffice are J. A. Kocher, A. T. Morris, J. C. Briggs, M. J. and J. I. Cook, I. N. Smith, J. M. Daran, L. Schrader, G. W. Brown and A. E. Koch.

CHILDS.

Is a postoffice situated in Green District, ten miles from the county seat, and three miles from the Short Line Railroad. It has one school house, and one M. E. church, the latter being situated on Laurel Point near the postoffice.

COBURN.

Is a postoffice situated in Grant district. There is no town nor village there more than a postoffice. U. B. Ice is postmaster.

DEAN.

Is a postoffice situated ten miles from the county seat in Green district. It was settled in the year of 1831 by John Strasinder and Thomas Bartlett, who came to that place and erected a cabin near the present site of the John Clark property. The town has one Christian church, one school house and one store. The store is owned by John Cullinan. Patrick Clark is the postmaster. Among the prosperous farmers around the town are J. J. Morris, T. P. Horner, Patrick Clark B. B. Postlethwait, J. A. Cumberledge Wm. Sapp, Alex. Sapp, Isaac Kirkpatrick, Morgan Wright and A. T. Cain.

JOHN DEBOLT,
Commissioner of the County Court.

HON. AARON MORGAN,
Present Member of Legislature from Wetzel County.

HUNDRED.

Is a town situated on the B. and O. R. R. and Fish creek, and has a population of 300. The first settlement was made by Old Hundred (see Henry Church) who patented the land on and around the town in 1819. The town has one church and one school house; four dry goods and notion stores, owned by D. Franklin & Sons, who also have a millinery department, Arnold & Allen, and A. D. Ayres, Martin Windle, Mrs. L. D. Roberts and Mr. Wiley; one millinery store, owned by Mrs. A. E. Lahew; two drug stores, owned by John McComas and Dr. Kerns; one barber shop, owned by W. W. Carpenter; one blacksmith shop, owned by F. Shultz ;and one hotel, Commercial house, W. H. Lee, proprietor. The town is furnished with gas. F. B. Hamilton now owns a large potrion of the Church patent. The first store in Hundred was opened by F. M. Kellar in 1886, and associated wiwth him was W. E. Hamilton. This store was located opposite the present postoffice, and is now under the management of D. Franklin & Sons. In 1894 T. B. Hamilton had a series of lot sales, in which a number were sold, and added a great deal to the prosperity of the town.

PADEN'S VALLEY.

Paden's Valley was settled in the year of 1790, by Obadiah Paden. He was among the first settlers of the Ohio Valley. He patented about two thousand acres of land, which at present bear his name. The extension of the Valley out in the country is known as Paden's Fork. The island in the Ohio river, lying in front of the Valley, containing about one hundred acres of land, is known as Paden's Island. He was of Dutch descent, and was originally from New York, later settling on the Susquehanna river, and was driven from there to the Valley. He erected a log house on a bank overlooking the beautiful Ohio, and taking up his large tract of land, he went to work with energy and determination, the chief characteristics of the old Dutch settlers. He was the father of about twelve children, the four sons chiefly inheriting the land of their father, and are known as Jesse, James, Joseph, and Samuel, who remain, and one daughter lies buried in the Paden cemetery. The remains of Obadiah Paden and his wife are both buried in the Paden cemetery and their grave is marked by a rough sandstone, the inscription being almost erased by time. There are two Indian mounds in the valley, one in the lower part, on the old Richard Ankrom farm. Many relics have been taken from these mounds. The town has one store, owned by Frank Boston. Annie Stephens is postmistress. Among the prosperous farmers around the town are Richard Ankrom, Mrs. Henry Ankrom, E. A. Pollack, James Stephens, J. N. Van Camp, A. J. Van Camp, L. Cook, Geo. Kiefer, Mr. Farmer, Geo. Smith and Uriah Kimble.

CHRISTIAN CHURCH.
New Martinsville

ARCHER'S FORK.

It was named from Archibald Woods, who patented a survey of land, which consisted of 6,000 acres in the year of 1796. The first permanent settler was William Ice, who took up about one hundred acres of land and erected a long cabin on it in the year of 1815, (the land is now owned by Emilia Shrew) and later his son, Abraham Ice, took up a tract of land which consisted of one hundred and twenty acres, where the present towns of Arches is now situated, and the farm is now owned by his grandson J. H. Dawson. Near the town the first oil well that was drilled in the county was located, being the well known as the Robinson No. 2, and was drilled by David McCain for the South Penn Oil Co., in 1893, and is still producing oil. The largest well in the county is also situated there, known as the Robinson No. 33. The town has two school houses, two churches (Methodist and Christian), and one store owned by Carlin Brothers. Among the prosperous farmers around the town are L. G. Robinson, J. H. Dawson, Carlin Brothers, William Springer, Isaac Shreves, and J. A. Edgel. The town is situated on the Short Line Railroad.

Note—The author is indebted to William Carlin for information concerning the early settlement of Arches.

PINE GROVE.

Is a town situated on Big Fishing creek and the Short Line Railroad. It has a population of about 500. The first settlement was made by Morgan Morgan (Spy Mod), who came to that place about the year of 1804, and erected a cabin on the present site of the livery stable, owned by Hennen. He also erected a grist mill near the saw and flour mill of Joliffe Bros. Other early settlers about Pine Grove were James Joliffe, Uriah Morgan and Mr. Wilson. The town took its name from a beautiful grove that at one time stood near the town; it has one school house, one church (Baptist), one clothing store, owned by Gooldfoos Brothers, one dry goods store, owned by J. W. Brookfield; one meat market, owned by W. J. Wharton & Sons; one barber shop, owned by Frank Myers; two blacksmith shops, owned by Cook Brothers, and Halbert & Co.; one hardware store, owned by Thomas Bucher; one general store, owned by William Long; one harness shop, owned by Dave Renner; two bakerys, owned by J. G. Wallace and Meck Piazzro; three grocery stores, owned by J. Brookfield, McQuain and Stone Brothers; three hotels, owned by Roome & Garvey, Mrs. Garvey and Mrs. Burley. The place has three doctors, Dr.'s Stone, Depew and McCluskey.

READER.

Reader is a town situated fifteen miles east of the county seat. It has a population of about one hundred. The first settlement was made in the year of 1788, by James Troy, who erected a cabin on what is now known as the negro quarters. He afterward sold his title to Benjamin Reader for a ten gallon copper kettle and a bay mare. The title consisted of six hundred acres. He afterwards sold his title to Morgan Morgan (Spy Mod) for a flint lock gun, and erected a cabin on what is known as the negro quarters, which got its name from him. He had negro slaves and had them stay on the place while he was living at what is now Pine Grove. The cabin was erected in 1804 and stood until 1896, when John Lantz, who owned the property, had it taken down. Several other men came to that neighborhood; among them were Jasper Strait, who moved in the same house with Morgan Morgan; William Snodgrass, Benjamin Hays, Thomas Bowl and James Booth, and Jacob Swisher. The pioneer school teacher of that neighborhood was Caleb Headlee, who taught in a six by ten log house. Morgan Morgan was lawed from the land by Jeremiah Williams, who was surveyor at the time, who sold it to Alexander Lantz, who transferred the land to John, the present owner. The land west of the negro quarters was patented by Zachwell Cochran in 1792. It consisted of 500 acres of the best farming land in the county and he lived upon this land until 1814, when he died, and the land became the property of his son, James Cochran, who died in 1893. When the land became the property of his heirs, who consisted of Jacob, A. S., Zachwell, Oliver, J. C., B. F., and Irvin Cochran, Druzela Hart, Margaret

Cook Emiline Millburn and Frances T. Long. John Millburn patented 200 acres south of the Cochran patent, lying on the waters of Brush run, in 1800. The land is now owned by W. M. Milburn and Martha Britton, who are living in the cabin that he erected in 1800. Among the prosperous farmers around Reader are Joseph Fair, George Sturge, Z. J. Morgan, John Springer, Stephen Brown, Samuel Springer, Oliver Cochran, Wm. Burgess, Rev. J. W. Gadd, W. A. Headlee, H. D. King, Benjamin Fox. J. D. Wayne, Wm. Kennedy, Wm. Kirkman, Louis Connely, Solomon Workman, Wm. and John Connely, C. Kidder, John McCalaster, N. Harris, James Harris, J. Springer, Chas. McCalaster, J. and R. Crosgry, Sam'l Harrison Sam Leap, Foster Clark, also hotel man and merchant, James Cochran, Presley Q. Martin and Harvey King.

SMITHFIELD.

Is a town situated thirty-one miles east of New Martinsville. It has a population of about 1,200. The first settlement was made by Aiden Bales in the year of 1796. It has three hotels, Brown Front, J. A. Davis, proprietor; the Shuman, M. D. Shuman, proprietor; and the Wilson, D. W. Wilson, proprietor. It has four dry goods and notion stores, owned by D. Carmichael, Howard and Calvert, L. G. Robinson, and W. A. Smith; one confectionery and news stand owned by T. J. Connely, and one barber shop, owned by Morris Sheon; the South Penn Oil Company has an office here; one blacksmith shop, owned by Geo. Beechman, and one meat market, owned by B. C. Ruggles. Among the prosperous farmers around the town are A. J. Slider, James Gump, F. C. Hays, H. S. Hays, L. Johnson, Henry Johnson, O. B. McIntire, C. A. Headlee, William Barker, Sr., William Barker, Jr., Charles Gilbert, J. J. Jackson, William Brewer, L. F. Cain, I. D. Morgan, Jas. A. Edgel, C. W. Ezra, and Grant Edgel, E. E. Ice, T. V. Ice, Dave Shuman, Henry and Levi Shuman, P. Minor, W. A. Wade, James A. Wade, H. J. Miller, C. S. Lowe, J. W., J. T., and H. Headlee, Gus and William Wyatt, Mrs. W. P. Morris, Louis and L. Morris, Morris L. Wyatt, Richard, J. M., and Johnson Anderson, I. Ice, F. Price, Oliver Bates, Curtis and Dawson Lemasters, L. G. Robinson, H. L. Smith, Geo. Hannan, Marion Shrieves, John and J. L. Welch, Jasper, George and Jackson Shrieves, David Ice, Albert, Sam and Dulin Edgel, L. E. and S. R. Cain, William Taylor, James Lively, John Leach, John Francis, John Showalter, William Carlin, Nelson Myres, John and Wash Carroll.

BURTON.

Burton is a town situated twenty-five miles east of New Martinsville, the county seat; it is situated on Fish creek and the B. & O. R. R. It has a population of about 250. It was settled by George Bartrug, whose father came to what is now known as Cottontown in the year of 1810, and erected a cabin on the land now owned by his heirs, Geo. Bartrug. After living with his parents for a short time, in 1812 erected a cabin on the site of the B. & O. R. R. The name of Burton should have been Bartrug, and it is presumed that when the name of what was then a landing place was given to the railroad company, that they took the name to be Burton. Peter Bartrug's patent consisted of 250 acres, which took in both Burton and Cottontown. Other settlements were made around Burton, of whom were Daniel Bartrug, brother of George, Peter Colwell and John Soles. Thomas Dawson was also a very early settler.

It has two dry goods and notion stores, of whom are Hennen & White, W. W. Robinson and John A. Hoge; one millinery store, Mrs. Dr. Lemley, proprietor; one blacksmith shop, W. S. Barrick, proprietor; one barber shop, owned by John Mallery; one flour mill, owned by John A. Hoge; one livery barn, owned by T. V. Ross; it has two hotels, the Central, owned by T. V. Ross, the Commercial, owned by Mrs. A. Homer. E. E. Cunningham is postmaster.

M. E. CHURCH. SOUTH.

VINCEN.

Was settled in the year of 1865 by Levi Merrett who is still living on a part of the land where he made the settlement. The place has one store, owned by Andrew Rice. Among the prosperous farmers around the town are A. J. Rice, David Founds, Vincent Amos and Levi Merett, J. T. Blair, Thomas Burgess, Ned Carroll Henry Egan, E. W Lemasters, J. S. Cross. I. J. Workman is the postmaster.

PROCTOR.

Is a town situated on the Ohio river and the Ohio River Railroad. It was settled at an early date by Jacob Moore, a carpenter and cabinet maker, who came to that place and erected
a cabin near the present site of the steamboat landing place.
The town, like the district, was named from a man by the
name of Proctor, who was the first to own the land where Proctor now stands. The town has two churches, Methodist and
Christian; one school house, three dry goods and notion stores,
owned by Todd & Whipkey, Monroe and Miller, and J. A. Dop-
ler; one hotel owned by Fleming Brothers; one barber shop,
owned by John Young; one blacksmith shop, owned by Charles
Oblinger, who also owns a hardware store; one harness shop
owned by K. Gates, two livery and feed stables, owned by Jas.
Fitzsimmons and A. C. Ruby; one machine shop, owned by
William Lee and one flour mill, owned by Watson Brothers.
J. F. Watson is postmaster. The town has one doctor, Dr.
Haught. Among the prosperous farmers around the town are
John Price, W. F. Moore, John Newman, William Lowrey A.
H. Haught, Friend Parsons, Israel Parsons, John Moore, Jacob
Yoho, M. and A. J. Moore.

EDUCATION OF WETZEL COUNTY, OF THE PIONEERS AND THE PRESENT DAY.

The children of the pioneers had very few educational advantages. The settlers were so poor that they could scarcely afford the small tuition. As soon as the children were able to travel the long distance usually required they were able to assist the father in clearing the land or the mother in her arduous tasks. Occasionally an itinerant schoolmaster found his way into a neighborhood, and for a few dollars he was engaged to instruct the youths for a period of two or three months. If an unoccupied dwelling house could be secured, it was furnished with a few long benches, made by splitting a small sapling and after smoothing one side slightly, holes were bored in the ends and pins inserted. Boards were placed on pins in the walls for writing desks. A three legged stool or block of wood was prepared for the teacher. The room was heated by a large fireplace, usually occupying the greater part of one end of the house.

The boys cut and carried the wood during the noon hour. Quite frequently the boys who attended these schools had to walk a distance of five miles and before starting for school in the morning two or three hours of work had to be done at home and a like number on his return. Those were days wnen "Jack" found no time for play. From such surroundings sprang the founders of our government.

The teachers of those days deserve much credit, for they certainly engaged in the work for the love they had for it. The remuneration was very meager. They "boarded around," that is, a week or two with one of their patrons and then with an.

other.   It did not take long for the teacher at that time to pack
his belongings and change his boarding place.   Besides assist-
ing the children with their work at night the "master" was expected to help do the chores in the evening and on Saturdays
take the ax or grubbing hoe and make a hand with the farmer.
By reason of this method of boarding the pioneer teacher understood his patrons and pupils better than do the teachers of
to-day.

The school boy of that day was not made "bandy legged" by
carrying a load of books.   Instruction was given only in the
three R's, Readin', Ritin', and Rithmetic; that was just about
all the "master" could teach; but that served to lay the
foundation of the men who conducted the business of the county for many years.

In 1864 the Free School System was inaugurated in Wetel
county.   At that time no school houses were found, but the
majority of the people were alive to their best interest and
buildings began to be located.   These were built of hewed logs.
The fire place gave place to the wood stove and the long-slab-
backless benches were replaced by the straight-backed seats.

The demand for better equipped teachers was made.   Teachers were scarce.   The schools were generally supplied from
Ohio and Pennsylvania.   It was soon found that there was tal-
ent at home, and the young men and women of Wetzel county
birth began to "wield the birch."

The last log school house has disappeared.   It was burned
down in 1900.   Every community is furnished with a comparatively comfortable building, furnished with the patent seats.
Not a child in the county is beyond reach of a school house.
In 1900 there were 135 buildings, employing 154 teachers.   The
enumeration of the school youth that year was 6,982; enroll-
ment, 6.010; average attendance, 3,647.

The teachers are paid according to the grade of certificate.
The average wages for No. 1 in 1900 was $31 1-7; No. 2, $27 2-7;
No. 3, $18 4-7.   The average school term was 5 1-6 months. Can

we look at these figures calmly and considerately without say-
ing that something must be done for the young men and women
who are devoting their best energies to the noble work of
teaching? Is it any wonder the teacher is using the profession
as a stepping stone?

The finnancial condition of the schools is good. In 1900, the
teachers' fund had a balance in the hands of the sheriff of
$2,968.52; the building fund, $2,731.16.

The county superintendents have been among our leading
educators; such as U. G. Morgan, Dr. Thos. Haskins, C. A. Mc-
Allister, John S. Wade, W. T. Sidell, L. W. Dulaney, and the
present incumbent, F. W. Parsons, who is serving his second
term.

The Magnolia Hig School is the only high school in the county. It was established under the general law for the estab-
lishment of high schools in 1880. The school is a district high
school; that is, persons living anywhere in Magnolia District
may send children entitled to enter the Intermediate Grammar
or High schools.

The high school course of study was prepared by E. E. Um
stead and adopted by the Board of Education October, 1887.
It has been several times revised, and at present is as follows:

JUNIOR CLASS.

Algebra—Ray's Elementary completed.

Arithmetic—Ray's Higher completed.

Grammar—Harvey's.

Civics—First and second terms.

Book-keeping—Last term.

Physiology—Cutter's Comprehensive.

Spelling—Reed and Kellogg's completed to page 113.

MIDDLE CLASS.

Spelling—Reed and Kellogg's to page 153.

Algebra—Ray's Higher completed to Ratio and Proportion.

Rhetoric—Hill's completed.

Physical Geography—Houston's first and second terms.

Mental Arithmetic—Completed.

General History—Myer's completed.

Latin—Chase and Stuart.

SENIOR CLASS.

Spelling—Reed and Kellogg completed.

Geometry—Wentworth's Plane completed.

Latin—Four books of Caesar's Gallic War.

Physics—Avery.

English and American Literature.

The following persons have been principal of the school: A. F. Wilmoth, S. B. Hall, S. W. Martin, Frank Burley, E. E. Umstead, J. N. Van Camp, W. W. Cline, J. M. Skinner, D. W. Shields, W. E. Maple, B. H. Hall and W. J. Postlethwait.

The high school library is composed of 905 well selected volumes. The school is supplied with $250 of laboratory apparatus.

AN INDIAN MASSACRE NEAR THE BORDERS OF WETZEL COUNTY.

On the 5th of December, 1787, a party of Indians and one white man, Leonard Schoolcraft, came into the settlement on Hoker's creek, and meeting with the daughter of Jesse Hughes, took her prisoner; passing on they came upon an old man by the name of West. He was carrying some fodder to the stable, and they likewise took him captive and carried him to where Hughes' daughter had been left in charge of some of the party. Here the old man got down on his knees and prayed fervently that they would not deal harshly with him, on which he was answered by a stroke of a tomahawk, which sent him to death's eternal sleep.

They then went to the house of the old man's son, Edmund West, where were Mrs. West and her sister, who was but eleven years old, daughter of John Hoker and a brother of West, a lad of twelve years. They forced open the door, Schoolcraft and two of the savages entered and one of them immediately tomahawked Mrs. West. The boy was taking some corn from under the bed and was drawn out by his feet and tomahawked. The girl was standing behind the door and one of the savages made toward her and aimed a blow at her head. She tried to evade it, but it struck her on the side of the neck, though not with sufficient force to knock her down. She fell, however, and lay as if killed. Thinking their work of death accomplished here, they took from a press some milk, butter and bread and placed it on the table and sat down to eat. The little girl observed all that was happening in silent stillness. When they had satisfied their hunger they arose, scalped the woman and boy, plundered the house, and departed, dragging the little girl by the hair about fifty yards from the house. They then threw her over a fence and scalped her, but as she evinced symptoms of life, Schoolcraft exclaimed, "That is not enough," when immediately a savage thrust a knife into her side, and they left her. Fortunately the point of the knife came in contact with a rib and did not injure her much.

Old Mrs. West and her two daughters were alone when the old gentleman was taken. They became uneasy that he did not return, and fearing that he had fallen into the hands of the savages, they left the house and went to the house of one Alexander West, who was then on a hunting expedition with his brother Edmund. They told them of the absence of the old man and their fears of his fate, and as there was no man here they went over to the house of Jesse Hughes, who was also uneasy as to the absence of his daughter, and on hearing that West, too, was missing, he did not doubt Mrs. West's predictions, and knowing of the absence of the younger West he deemed it advisable to apprize his wife of danger and re-move her to his house. On which he started toward the house, accompanied by Mrs. West and her two daughters. On en-tering the door a horrible spectacle was presented to their view. Mrs. West and the lad lay upon the floor welting in their blood, but not yet dead. The sight overpowered the girls, and Hughes had to carry them off. Seeing that the savages had just left them, and aware of the danger that they would be menaced with if the alarm be given to the Indians, Hughes guarded his own house that night and in the morning spread the sorrowful news of the massacre, and organized a company of men who went in pursuit of the Indians and to try to find the missing ones. Young West was found, standing in the creek about a mile from home, where he had been toma-hawked. The brains were oozing from his head, yet he sur-vived in extreme suffering for three days. Old Mr. West was found in the field where he had been tomahawked. Mrs. West probably lived but a few minutes after Hughes and her sisters-in-law had left there. The little girl (Hoker's daughter) was found in bed at the home of old Mr. West. She related the story to Edmund West, and said that she went to sleep, when she was thrown over the fence and was awakened by the scalping. After she had been stabbed, at the suggestion of Schoolcraft, and left, she tried to re-cross the fence to the house, but as she was climbing up she again went to sleep and fell back. After awakening she walked into the woods and sheltered herself as good as she could in the top of a tree and remained until morning.

Remembering that there was no person left alive at her sister's house, she proceeded to go to the house of old man West. She found no person at home, the fire nearly out, but the hearth warm. She laid down on it, but the ashes produced a sickening odor which caused her to get up and go to bed, where she was found. She recovered, grew up and was married, and gave birth to ten children. She died, as was believed by many, from an affection of the head, caused by the wound she received that night. Hughes' daughter was ransomed by her father the next year, and for a long time lived in sight of the theatre of those savage enormities.

THE HEROISM OF MRS. BOZARTH.

An Incident of Border Warfare in Monongalia County.

After the combat of Capt. David Morgan and the two savages the alarm caused the settlers of the neighborhood of
Prickett's Fort to gather at the house of Mrs. Bozarth for
safety, and on the 1st of April, 1778, when only Mrs. Bozarth
and two men were in the house, the children, who were out at
play, came running toward the house in full speed, exclaiming
that there were "ugly red men coming." Upon hearing this,
one of the two men in the house went to the door to see if
Indians really were coming, and received a glancing shot on
his breast, which caused him to fall back. The Indian who
had shot him sprang in immediately after, and grappled with
the other white man, and was quickly thrown on the bed. His
antagonist having no weapon with which to do him any injury.
called to Mrs. Bozarth for a knife. Not finding one at hand, she
seized an axe, and at one blaw let out the brains of the pros-
trate savage. By this time another savage entered the door
and shot dead the man engaged in combat with his companion. Mrs. Bozarth turned on him and with a well directed
blow knocked him in the head and caused him to call out for
help. Upon this the others who were engaged with the children in the vard, came to the door, and as each one would stick
his head in the door he would be sent to the happy huntinʊ
grounds by the hand of Mrs. Bozarth. The children in the
yard were all killed and one of the men, but by the coolness
and infinite self-possession of Mrs. Bozarth she succeeded in
saving her own life and that of the man who was first shot, and
keeping the savages from taking possession of the house.

AN INDIAN MASSACRE IN TYLER COUNTY.

In August, 1787, five Indians on their way to the Indian settlement on the Monongahela river met two men on Middle Island creek, Tyler county, and killed them. Taking the dead men's horses the continued their journey until they came to the house of William Johnson, on what is now known as "Ten Mile," and made prisoners of Mrs. Johnson and some children; plundered the house, killed part of the stock, and taking with them one of Johnson's horses, returned toward the Ohio. When the Indians came to the house Johnson had gone to a Lick not far off, and on his return in the morning, seeing what had been done, and searching until he found the trail of the savages and their prisoners, ran to Clarksburg for assistance. A company of men repaired with him immediately to where he had discovered the trail, and keeping it about a mile, found four of the children lying upon the ground dead and scalped. and their bodies laid in a form as to represent a cross. The dead were buried and further pursuit given over.

ADAM POE'S FAMOUS FIGHT WITH BIG FOOT.

Some time near the year of 1780, a party of Wyandotts consisting of five of the most distinguished chiefs of that nation, came into one of the intermediate settlements between Fort Pitt and Wheeling and killed an old man, who was alone in the vast wilderness, and robbed him of all that was in the cabin. After doing this, they commenced retreating with the plunder, but they were soon discovered by spies, among whom were Andrew and Adam Poe, two brothers, distinguished for their build, physical strength and bravery, who went in pursuit of them, coming near them not far from the Ohio river. Adam Poe, fearing that the Indians were in ambush, left his companions, where he started toward the river under cover of the high grass, with a few to attack them unawares, should they be in such a position. At last he saw an Indian raft at the edge of the water, but saw no Indians; presently he walked cautiously through the grass, and had gone but a few steps when he saw below him under the bank the big Wyandott chief, "Big Foot," and a little Indian side by side, muttering something in a very low tone, and watching the party of whites who were lower down the bottom. Poe then raised his gun to shoot, aiming at the big chief; the gun snapped, which betrayed his presence; seeing no chance for retreat, he immediately sprang upon the big chief, and seizing him by the breast and at the same time putting his arm around the neck of the smaller Indian, threw them both to the gorund, knocking the two Indians senseless for the time being. They then struggled for a while, on which the smaller Indian succeeded in getting loose from the grasp of Poe, and af course, as soon as he got free grabbed a tomahawk and started toward Poe, but a vigor-

ous and well-idrected kick soon put an end to the Indian's intentions for a while; but after recovering from the shock he
had received by the kick, the Indian again raised his tomahawk, but this time Poe saved himself by throwing up his
arms, as the blow was aimed at his head. Poe now realized that
he was menaced by a terrible danger, and freeing himself from
the grip of the chief, he arose, picked up a gun and shot the
smaller Indian through the stomach. By this time the big
chief had regained his feet, and seizing Poe by the shoulder
and leg threw him up in the air like a man would throw a small
baby. Poe, however, was soon on his feet, and engaged in a
close struggle. By this time they were both at the water's
edge; the question now was to drown the other, and the efforts
to accomplish this were continued for a long time without any
success. At last Poe grasped the long hair of the chief and
held him under the water until he thought he was dead and
relaxed his hold, but too soon; in an instant the gigantic savage was again on his feet and ready for another combat. In
this they were both taken beyond their depth and had to swim
for safety; both swam for all their might toward the shore.
The Indian was a more expert swimmer and succeeded in
reaching the shore first. By this time Andrew Poe (his brother), who had just returned from a conflict with the other
members of the band, killing all but one, getting worried about
his brother, went in search of him and there appeared in the
nick of time to save his brother. Adam, seeing that the Indian would reach shore first, turned and swam back into the
river, thinking that he could get beyond the reach of the gun
of the heartless savage, and some other member of the gang
taking him for an Indian, shot and wounded him severely. He
then called upon his brother to shoot the big Indian on the
shore, which he did, and immediately sprang into the river after his brother, who was so severely hurt that he could not
swim. The wounded chief then rolled into the river to save
a trophy that is so dear to every Indian warrior.

SAD DEATH OF CAPTAIN VAN BUSKIRK.

Early in June, 1792, occurred the last conflict on the upper Ohio, between an organized party of Virginians and Indians. In consequence of the numerous depredations on the settlements now embraced in Brooke and Hancock counties, it was determined to summarily chastise these marauders; and, accordingly, a party of men organized under the command of Captain Van Buskirk, an officer of tried courage and acknowledged efficiency. A party of Indians had committed sundry acts of violence, and it was believed they would endeavor to cross the Ohio, on their retreat, at some point near Mingo Bottom. Van Buskirk's party consisted of about forty experienced frontiersmen, some of whom were veteran Indian hunters. The number of the enemy was known to be about thirty.

The whites crossed the river below the mouth of Cross Creek, and marched up the bottom, looking cautiously for the enemy's trail. They had discovered it along the run, but missing, concluded to take the ridge, hoping thus to cross it. Descending the ridge, and just as they gained the river, the Indians fired upon them, killing Captain Van Buskirk and wounding John Aidy.

The enemy were concealed in a ravine amidst a dense cluster of paw paw bushes. The whites marched in single file, headed by their Captain, whose exposed situation will account for the fact that he was riddled with thirteel balls. The ambush quartered on their flank, and they were totally unsuspicious of it. The plan of the Indians was to permit the whites to advance in numbers along the line before firing upon them. This was done; but instead of each selecting his man, every gun was directed at the Captain, who fell with thirteen bullet-holes in his body. The whites and Indians instantly treed, and contest lasted more than an hour. The Indians, however. were defeated, and retreated towards the Muskingum, with the loss of several killed; while the Virginians, with the exception of their Captain, had none killed, and but three wounded.

Captain Van Buskirk's wife was killed just eleven months previous to the death of her husband. They lived about three miles from West Liberty. She had been taken prisoner by the Indians, and on their march towards the river her ankle was sprained so that she could not walk without pain. Finding her an incumbrance, the wretches put her to death on the hill just above where Wellsville now stands. On the following day her body was discovered by a party who had gone out in pursuit.

MURDER OF THE TWO MISSES CROW.

Next to the Tush murder, perhaps the most melancholy oc-currence on Wheeling Creek was that of two sisters—the Misses Crow, which occurred in 1785. The parents of these girls lived about one mile above the mouth of Dunkard, or lower fork of the creek. According to the statement of a third sister, who was an eye-witness to the horrid tragedy and her-self almost a victim, the three left their parents' house for an evening walk along the deeply-shaded banks of that beautiful stream. Their walk extended over a mile and they were just turning back, when suddenly several Indians sprang from be-hind a ledge of rocks and seized all three of the sisters. With scarcely a moment's interruption, the savages led the captives a short distance up a small bank when a halt was called and a parley took place. It seems that some of the Indians were in favor of immediate slaughter, while others were disposed to carry them into permanent captivity.

Unfortunately, the arm of mercy was powerless. Without a moment's warning, a fierce-looking savage stepped from the group, with elevated tomahawk, and commenced the work of death. This Indian, in the language of the surviving sister, "Began to tomahawk one of my sisters—Susan by name. Su-san dodged her head to one side, the tomahawk taking effect in her neck, cutting the jugular vein, the blood gushing out a yard's length. The Indian who held her hand jumped back to avoid the blood. The other Indian then began the work of death on my sister Mary.

I gave a sudden jerk and got loose from the one that held me and ran with all speed, taking up a steep bank, but just as I caught hold of a bush to help myself up, the Indian fired and the ball passed through the clump of hair on my head, slightly breaking the skin. I gained the top in safety the Indian tak-ing round in order to meet me as I would strike the path that led homeward. But I ran right from home and hid myself in the bushes near the top of the hill. Presently I saw an Indian passing along the hill below me; I lay still until he was out of sight; I then made for home."

FOURTH JUDICIAL CIRCUIT.

The Home of Thrift, Enterprise and Industry in the State of West Virginia.
Its Wonderful Past, Its Present and Future—A Great and Progressive
Country, With Pen Pictures of the People Who Have and Are Con-
tributing to Her Industrial, Financial, Mercantile and Commercial
Importance—Some Facts About Tyler County.

In the study of the history of the Fourth Judicial Circuit it
is necessary that we understand something of the causes which
have acted in producing and advancing or retarding and de-
stroying, the various institutions, civil and otherwise, of the
Commonwealth. That we may study intelligently the history
of West Virginia—"The Little Mountain State," the "Daughter
of the Old Dominion," born amid the throes of civil war—it is
important that we look to the causes which have led to its settlement and organization as a State.

In 1634, twenty-seven years after the founding of Jamestown,
Virginia was divided into eight counties or shires similar to
those in England. These, the first in the New World, were
named James City, Henrico, Elizabeth City, Warwick River,
Warrosquyoake—now Isle of Wight—Charles River and Aco-
mack. Virgil A. Lewis, who wrote a history of West Virginia,
says: "Virginia ever tried to keep civil government abreast of
her most adventurous pioneers, and to accomplish this, her
House of Burgesses continued to make provision for the formation of new counties. After the eight original ones came others in the order named: Northampton and Gloucester, in 1642;
Northumberland, in 1648; Surry and Lancaster, in 1652; West-
moreland, in 1653; Sussex and New Kent, in 1654; Stafford and
Middlesex, in 1675; Norfolk, Princess Anne, and King and

AN OIL DERRICK.

Queen, in 1691; Richmond, in 1692; King William, in 1701·
Prince George, in 1702; Spottsylvania, King George, Hanover
and Brunswick, in 1720; Goochland and Caroline, in 1727;
Amelia and Orange, in 1734; Augusta, in 1738; Albemarle, in
1744; Amherst, in 1761; and Botetourt, in 1769.

From 1732 to 1750 many pioneers found homes in the Opequon, Back Creek, Little and Great Cacapon and South Branch
Valleys. These settlements were made principally within the
present limits of Jefferson, Berkeley, Morgan and Hampshire
counties and were the earliest in West Virginia. Quite a number of those who settled in Berkeley and Jefferson were Quak-
ers, and to them is due the credit of being established the first
religious organization, not only in West Virginia, but west of
the Blue Ridge. That they had regular meetings as early as
1738, is proven conclusively by a letter written by Thomas
Chauckley on May 21, 1738, and addressed to "The Friends of
the Monthly Meeting at Opequon."

A century and a half have passed away since the first white
men found homes in West Virginia. It is not a long time, yet,
when they came Washington was an infant in his mother's
arms; no Englishmen had been on the banks of the Ohio; no
white man had found a home within the confines of Georgia;
New Hampshire was a part of Massachusetts, the French had
a cordon of forts extending from the St. Lawrence to the Mississippi and savage tribes roamed all over the country from
the Blue Ridge to the Pacific. It was five years before the
founding of Richmond, 23 years before the French and Indian
war, and 43 years before the Revolution. Truly this is the old
part of West Virginia.

At the beginning of the Revolution but two of the counties
of West Virginia had an existence. These were Berkeley and
Hampshire. In 1775 the former extended from the Blue Ridge
to the Ohio, while the latter stretched away from the North
mountain to the western limit. South of Hampshire lay Augusta county, reaching from the Blue Ridge to the Ohio, and

including all territory between the Little Kanawha and Great Kanawha rivers, while all that part of the State lying south of the latter was included within the bounds of Fincastle county. The district of West Augusta was all that territory west of the mountains, the boundaries of which as defined in 1776, included all the territory west of the mountains, the boundaries of which as defined in 1776, included all the territory north of Middle Is-land Creek, and lying west and south of the Monongahela river to the Ohio. During the Revolution a small rebellion broke out in the Augusta district, and this insurrection was known as "Claypole's Rebellion," as John Claypole, a Scot. was the leader. The trouble was caused by Claypole refusing to pay his taxes and getting others to join him in resisting the officers. He was finally arrested, some of his stock appropriated, and his band of insurgents broken up.

Concerning the Augusta district of West Virginia, of which Tyler county was a part, Washington once said during the darkest period of the Revolution: "Leave me but a banner to place on the mountains of Augusta and I will rally around me the men who will lift our bleeding country from the dust and set her free.

Of the men who helped to free America, many of the best were from the hills and valleys of this part of West Virginia. Their names have been consigned to oblivion but their memory shall live as long as there is an American flag to wave over the land of the free and the home of the brave.

"When Augusta county was formed it included all of the 'ut-most parts of Virginia' and extended from the Blue Ridge mountains on the east to the Mississippi river on the west. From its original limits have been carved the States of West Virginia, Kentucky, Ohio, Indiana, Illinois and Michigan. Its western boundary was the French possessions of Louisiana.

Botetourt was formed from the southern part of Augusta, from which it was separated by a line drawn westward from the point at which the James river breaks through the Blue

BURNING OF AN OIL TANK.

Ridge, and terminating near the present site of Keokuk, on the Mississippi. In 1772, Fincastle county was formed from the southern part of Botetourt, but its existence was of short duration, for it was extinguished in 1776, by an act of the General Assembly, which created from its territory the counties of Montgomery, Washington and Kentucky, the boundaries being almost identical with those of the State now bearing its name.

"In 1778, Virginia made her first effort to establish civil government west of the Ohio river. In October of that year the Assembly passed an act creating the county of Illinois from Botetourt. It included all of Virginia west of the Ohio, by which it was bounded on the south and southeast; Pennsylvania lay on the east; the great lakes on the north; and the Mississippi washed its boundaries on the west. John Todd was appointed county lieutenant and civil commandant of Illinois county. He was killed at the battle of Blue Licks, in Kentucky, August 18, 1782, and his successor in office was Timothy de Monthbrunn.

"But Virginia's authority was not long to continue beyond the Ohio. On October 20, 1783, the Assembly passed an act entitled 'An act to authorize the delegates of this State in Congress assembled all the rights of this Commonwealth to the territory northwestward of the river Ohio.' This offer the United States accepted, and the deed of cession was promptly made March 22, 1784, and signed on the part of Virginia by Thomas Jefferson, Samuel Hardy, Arthur Lee and James Monroe, members of Congress from Virginia. This deed may be seen in "Henning's General Statutes," Vo. xi, p. 571.

Before entering upon the history of Wetzel county, it is proper to notice what was for some time known as the "District of West Augusta." The boundaries, which will be best understood by the reader with a map of the State before him, were defined by act of Assembly in 1776, as follows: "Beginning on the Alleghany mountains between the heads of the Potomac, Cheat and Greenbrier rivers; thence along the ridge of moun-

tains which divides the waters of Cheat river from those of
Greenbrier and that branch of the Monongahela river called
Tygart's Valley river, on the northwest of the said West Fork,
thence up the said creek to the head thereof; thence in a direct
course to the head of Middle Island creek, a branch of the Ohio
river; and thence to the Ohio including all the waters of the
aforesaid creek in the aforesaid District of West Augusta, all
that territory lying to the northward of the aforesaid boundary
and to the westward of the States of Pennsylvania and Maryland, shall be deemed and is hereby declared to be within the
boundaries of West Augusta."

The boundaries thus defined, if delineated on a map of the
present State, would begin on the summit of the Alleghanies
at the northwest corner of Pocahontas county, and run thence
southwest between that county and Randolph to Mingo Flat in
the latter, thence north through that county, thence northwest through Barbour and Taylor into Marion with the mean-
derings of Tygart's Valley river to its confluence with the Monongahela, thence up the West Fork of that river to the mouth
of Bingamon's creek in Harrison, and thence west with the
stream to its source.   And thence southwest through the latter
county to the head of Middle Island creek in Doddridge; thence
northwest centrally through that county and Tyler to the Ohio;
thence northeast with that river to the present site of Pittsburg; thence with the Monongahela and Cheat rivers through
the Southwestern part of Pennsylvania and Preston and Tucker
counties to the beginning.

The territory thus embraced included two-thirds of the county of Randolph, half of Barbour, a third of Tucker, half of Taylor, a third of Preston, nearly the whole of Marion, Monroe and
Monongalia, a fourth of Harrison, half of Doddridge, two-thirds
of Tyler, and the whole of Wetzel, Marshall, Ohio, Brooke and
Hancock in West Virginia, and the whole of Greene, Washington and parts of Allegheny and Beaver counties in Pennsylvania.

SCENE ON THE OHIO RIVER.

A succeeding section of the same act provided for the division of West Augusta into three counties, to be known as Ohio, Yohogania and Monongalia. By the westward extension of Mason and Dixon's line in 1784, the great part of Yohogania fell into Pennsylvania, and the remainder was by act of Assembly in 1785, added to Ohio county. Thus Yohogania became extinct.

Having thus noted the efforts of Virginia to establish civil government in her western domain, we proceed to Tyler county in detail.

Tyler county was formed from Ohio, by act of December 16, 1814, by which the boundaries were defined as follows: Beginning at the south and Pennsylvania line; thence a due west course to the Ohio river; thence with said river to the Wood county line; thence with said line to the line dividing Monongalia from Ohio county; thence with said line to the Pennsylvania line, and with it to the place of beginning. The commissioners to locate the seat of justice were Dudley Evans and Levi Morgan, of Monongalia, Moses Congleton and Samuel Chambers, of Brooke, and Benjamin Robinson and Davidson, Jr., of Harrison. The county was named in honor of John Tyler, who was born in James county, Virginia, February 28, 1747. He graduated at Williams and Marys college, then studied law in the office of Robert Carter Nicholas, at Williamsburg. He was long a member of the Assembly and commanded a body of Charles City troops during the Revolutionary war. In 1870 he became a member of the Council of State, and December 1, 1808, was elected Governor of Virginia. Before his term expired President Madison appointed him to the judgeship of the District Court of the United States for Virginia, in which capacity he served until his death January 6, 1813. He was the father of John Tyler, tenth President of the United States.

Middlebourne was established a town by legislative enactment January 27, 1813, on the lands of Robert Gorrell, then in Ohio county, and Wallace Wells, Sr., Joseph Martin, Joseph

Ardor, Thomas Grigg, Daniel Haynes, William Delashmult, and Abraham S. Brookhead, trustees.

The town was incorporated February 3, 1871. One of the first pioneers of the banks of the Ohio, below Wheeling, was Charles Wells, who settled near the present site of Sistersville in 1776. He was residing here in 1812 when a gentleman vis ited him and the same year published a work descriptive of the Ohio Valley. From it we extract the following:

"Charles Wells, Sr., resident on the Ohio river, fifty miles below Wheeling, related to me while at his house in October 12, the following circumstances: 'That he has had two wives (the last of which still lives and is hale, smart, young looking woman) and 22 children, 16 of whom are living, healthy, and many of them married and have already pretty large families. That a tenant of his, a Mr. Scott, a Marylander, is also the fa- ther of 22 children, the last being still an infant, and its mother a lively and gay Irish woman, being Scott's second wife. That a Mr. Gordon, an American German, formerly a neighbor of Mr. Wells, now residing on Little Muskingum, State of Ohio, has had by his two wives 28 children. Mr. Gordon is near 80 years old, active and hale in health.' " Thus these three wor- thy families have had born to them 72 children, a number un- exampled perhaps in any part of the world, and such as would make Buffon stare, when he ungenerously asserts, as do several other writers of Europe, that animal life degenerates in Amer- ica.

Tyler was the only West Virginia county created during the second war with Great Britain.

Sistersville, which was formerly only a ferry, was established from the lands of John McCoy January 28, 1818. The town was incorporated February 2, 1839.

BUILDING AN OIL TANK.

THE PHILIP G. BIER G. A. R. POST.

The Philip G. Bier G. A. R. Post was organized August 21, 1883, with the following charter members:

J. E. Hart,
J. E. Baker.
R. T. Richardson,
Wm. Schrouder
Elijah Morgan,
John Fowler,
Harmison Criswell,
N. Martin,
Geo. B. Woodcock,
W. H. Hitchcock,
T. B. Carothers,
Marshall Whiteman
Jas. Gardner,

C. L. Yager,
J. M. Francis,
Martin Buskirk,
Jas. Shriver,
W. H. McEldowney,
Bruce Briggs,
Jos. Cutshaver,
Basil T. Bowers,
Stephen Daugherty,
E. W. Lauck
T. M. Higgins,
G. H. Hitchcock
Frank Evans

C. D. Dolby.

The Past Commanders are as follows:

1. R. T. Richardson.
3. B. T. Bowers.
5. J. T. Rohrbaugh.
7. W. H. McEldowney.
9. G. B. Woodcock,

2. J. E. Hart.
4. Jas. Baker.
6. J. K. Gorby.
8. J. M. Francis.
10. F. C. Harvey.

11. Robt. McGee.

The present Commander is Thomas Mills.

F. C. Harvey is Adjutant.

WETZEL LODGE No. 39, A., F. & A. M.

Amont the secret orders having lodges in Wetzel county, a leading place must be given to Wetzel Lodge No. 39, Ancient. Free and Accepted Masons, of New Martinsville.

The first meeting of Wetzel Lodge U. D. was held July 28 1868, the Rev. R. A. Claughton, of Middlebourne Lodge No. 34. officiating as W. M. The first officers of the Lodge U. D. were as follows: John S. Monroe, Henry S. McCabe, Thomas Cellers. John H. Moore, John Snodgrass and William McMunn. The first work was done September 1, 1868, when John C. McEldowney, William W. Hall, John A. Shriver and John S. Rider were initiated. The first work in the third degree was October 6, 1868, when John C. McEldowney, Robert McEldowney, and William W. Hall were raised to the sublime degree of Master Mason. The first funeral service conducted by the Lodge was September 18, 1868, when William M. Bartlett was laid to rest.

The charter of Wetzel No. 39 is dated November 10th, 1869. and is signed by William J. Bates, Grand Master, and Thomas H. Logan, Grand Secretary. The Lodge was constituted January 25th, 1870, by Odell S. Long, the most eminent of West Virginia Free Masons, J. V. L. Rogers officiating as Grand Marshal. The first officers under the charter were as follows: John S. Monroe, John S. Rider, John C. McEldowney, Josephus Clark, George E. Boyd, William W. Hall and Thomas J. Hill. The first stated communication under the charter was held February 1st, 1870.

The following is a complete list of the Worshipful Masters of Wetzel Lodge No. 39: John S. Monroe, John S. Rider, B. M. Welch (three years in all), John C. McEldowney (two years), John Cherry, J. P. Dunlap, John McComas (two years), M. R.

FRANK WELLS CLARK,
W. M. of the Masons.

Crouse, Thomas Perry Jacobs (five years in all), F. C. Bucher (four years in all), F. E. McEldowney (two years), Robert Mc-Eldowney (three years), W. McG. Hall (three years), Frank W. Clark (three years).

For many years the Lodge met in the old Court House, torn down to make way for the new temple of justice now being erected by the county. About three years since the Lodge removed to its present pleasant quarters in the third floor of the McCaskey Building.

The Lodge membership at present is about one hundred, comprising many of the most prominent men of the town and county. The roster of Lodge officers for the year 1901 is as follows Frank W. Clark, W. M.; John W. Kaufman, S. W.; A. B. Morrison, J. W.; F. E. McEldowney, Treas.; James Bishop, Secretary; O. L. Haught, S. D.; L. V. McIntire, J. D.; William Debolt, Tiler; John Stamm and J. U. Dayton, Stewards; Rev. W. H. Burkhardt, Chaplain.

Perhaps the "biggest day" in the history of the Lodge was August 31st, 1900, on which date the corner stones of the new Wetzel county Court House and of the new M. E. church were laid under Masonic auspices, E. M. Turner officiating as Grand Master, and a large body of Knights Templar acting as escort for the Grand Lodge.

Wetzel Lodge has been a most important factor in the development of the county, and will continue so to be as long as its members cherish those bright jewels of the Order, "Friendship, Morality and Brotherly Love."

West Virginia Monumental Works.

We here present a fair likeness of Rev. T. H. Hawkins, Manager and sole owner of the West Virginia Monumental works.

REV. T. H. HAWKINS,
Manager of the W. Va. Monumental Works.

The West Virginia Monumental Works is situated at New Martinsville and is one of the largest concerns of its kind in the State. They work all kinds of marble and granite, having a steam power apparatus for polishing their work, both granite and marble. Twelve men are constantly employed at the works. C. W. Beck is foreman. The workmen are: Cutters. Holly Sayre, Roy Corbet, James McClain, James Debolt, Harry Hawkins and George Huff. Other workmen are Turner Wells, Quincy Moore, Earl McIntire, Frank Tarter and C. M. Mathes. J. A. Kramer is transfer man.

JACOB KOONTZ,
Of the firm of Koontz & Philips.

KOONTZ & PHILLIPS.

PLANING MILL.

The largest planing mill and lumber yard in the county is owned by Koontz and Philips, and is situated near the Ohio River R. R. on the Big Fishing creek bank. Charles Koontz is General Manager. The company employs thirty-eight men, of whom are J. Koontz and E. F. Philips, Thos. Fink, Arch Gilbert, Geo. Showalter, Sr., Geo. Showalter, Jr., Wm. Showalter. Harry Showalter, Ezra Daugherty, Theo. Clegg, Wm. Hammell. Dave Hammell, Charles Koontz, Harry Evans, Frank Waits, Jere Waits, Joseph Minor, Thos. Minor, Frank Workman, O. S. Beaver, Wm. Yager, Simon Potts, Frank Shaffer, Albert Rist, George Snodgrass, Chas. Enslow, Chas. Waits, John Harigan, Basil Hill, John Harman, Elias Gilbert, Wm. Findlay, L. Zessiger, W. W. Carr, Ury Minor, Carl Kappel, Robert Smith, Simon Brothers.

Made in the USA
Middletown, DE
20 December 2018